PLYMOUTH BYGONES

Sixty years of memories and pictures

Guy Fleming

DEVON BOOKS

First published in Great Britain in 1991 by Devon Books.
Copyright © 1991 Guy Fleming

British Library Cataloguing-in-Publication Data
Fleming, Guy
    Plymouth bygones: sixty years of memories and pictures.
    1. Devon. Plymouth, history
    I. Title
    942.358

ISBN 0 86114-854-1

Typeset by P&M Typesetting Ltd, Exeter

Printed and bound in Great Britain by Penwell Print Ltd, Callington

DEVON BOOKS
Official Publisher to Devon County Council
An imprint of Wheaton Publishers Ltd, a member of
Maxwell Communication Corporation plc

Wheaton Publishers Ltd
Hennock Road, Marsh Barton, Exeter, Devon EX2 8RP
Tel: 0392 411131; Fax: 0392 425274 Telex: 42794 (WHEATN G)

SALES
Direct sales enquiries to Devon Books at the address above.

ACKNOWLEDGEMENTS

Some parts of this book have previously appeared in the *Evening Herald*, and are reproduced here by kind permission of the Editor.

The following photographs are reproduced by kind permission of the City Museum and Art Gallery, Plymouth: pages 2 (bottom), 3, 14, 16, 30 (top), 34, 59 (top), 72 (Doris Goodridge collection), 78, 79, (Doris Goodridge collection), 81 (top, Doris Goodridge collection). Other photographs are from private collections.

The author wishes to thank Mr James Barber, Keeper of Human History at the City Museum and Art Gallery, Plymouth, for his sage advice and assistance.

CONTENTS

The beginnings of Old Laira Road at Lipson, with one of the many farmhouses which were swept away to make room for the town's expansion eastwards at the end of the last century. ▼

INTRODUCTION

Old Plymouth had a closeness and an intimacy which now lingers on only in fading memory; recollections of narrow streets and cobbled communal courtyards where washing flapped loosely in the breeze, still remain in the minds of those who mourn the loss of the old place.

Memory is often deceptive, though — and perhaps people tend to forget that the courtyards often were locked in shadows where a rare triangle of sunshine served only to illuminate clouds of flying dust. The rows of little houses in the first half of the century harboured darkness and disease; much of central Plymouth, Devonport and Stonehouse wore sad, tattered trimmings, a legacy of pathetic hovels hemmed in by factory walls, lacking space and clean air to breathe. Seventy years ago, one-third of the houses in Plymouth were from eighty to a hundred years old and, in some cases, there were more than 200 people per acre.

However, hard as times were for many, the city of the Edwardian era wore something of a jaunty air, as these reminiscences reveal. Pleasures could be had cheaply and life possessed a zest and gaiety that somehow became lost to later generations in their comparative affluence.

The citizens kept six theatres and (at one time) fifteen cinemas doing brisk business. The Great Western and Southern railways took passengers 'to all parts', from Millbay and Friary stations respectively. Steamers ran regularly to Millbrook and Saltash and, further up the Tamar, to Calstock, a favourite outing rendezvous in those seemingly torpid days before the First World War. A ferry and horse boats plied between Admiral's Hard and Cremyll, and once on the Cornish side of the river, passengers could go by Haddy's Bus to Kingsand, or by Skinner's Motor Bus to Cawsand or Millbrook.

There was also a ferry between Plymouth, Oreston and Turnchapel. By the mid 1920s there was a tram service on fifteen routes, besides the Plymouth Corporation Omnibus Service with its eleven routes, although there were no buses on Sundays before 2 p.m.

In spite of all the difficulties in those far-off days, so evocatively caught by those whose memories fill this book, local people were glad to call themselves Plymothians — part of the fabric of a lively, bustling seaport with a fiercely rich history, a sense of civic pride had never been wanting.

The Three Towns grew at an astonishing pace. In 1801 the total population of Plymouth was 19 000 and of Devonport 24 000 but, by the outbreak of the First World War, the combined population had reached 209 000.

The developing Laira suburb, facing the main London to Penzance railway line. These houses still stand and the area is known as the 'The Narrows'. ▶

Sunlight and washing in a yard behind cottages in Castle Dyke Lane; photographed in 1914. These cottages were pulled down in the 1930s in a slum clearance scheme to make way for council flats. ▶

Housing pressure resulted in gaps between and within the towns being infilled and spreading into adjoining rural areas. In Devonport, a suburb to serve Dockyard workers developed at Morice Town, while the villages of Lower and Higher Stoke knitted together as one. A syndicate of builders developed the Keyham Barton area, north of St Levan Road, while larger houses spread from Higher Stoke and Molesworth Road, joining developments from Millbridge to Pennycomequick. In 1898 Devonport took in St Budeaux and Pennycross, two years after Plymouth had absorbed parts of Compton, Weston Peverell, Eggbuckland and Laira.

Plymouth's growth had been limited by a large number of private estates, dictating development northwards to North Road and Cobourg Street, up to North Hill, down Alexandra Road and along Mutley Plain. Larger houses, for the growing professional classes, were erected from Mannamead to Hyde Park Corner, at the western end of Mutley Plain. By the early twentieth century the town was filled from Tothill to Lipson, Prince Rock to Cattedown, Mutley to Mannamead and to Peverell Park Road, while new developments reached into Beacon Park.

In 1914, the Three Towns were at last merged into one local authority, perhaps the most significant municipal landmark in their history. This step had been mooted for years and seemed inevitable. And once the Admiralty had made it clear that, in the event of war, they would sooner deal with a single authority, the pace dramatically quickened.

Sutton Harbour and the Barbican, the ancient core of the city, photographed before the end of the nineteenth century. ▼

An embryo city was in the making. When King George V at last issued his decree giving it that status, in October 1928, Plymouth was already a major county, municipal and parliamentary borough. Admittedly, it was less than a third of its present size; its boundaries enclosed 6075 acres compared with today's 20 000. In 1938, Crownhill came within its ambit. After the Second World War further outlying territory was incorporated, first of all at Tamerton Foliot (1950), and then the strongly-resented take-over of Plympton and Plymstock in 1967.

This was fought tenaciously by the two authorities, particularly Plympton which was 'in business' years before its newer neighbour. Petitions were scattered about like confetti, protests were mounted to the House of Commons but all to no avail as Richard Crossman, then Local Government minister, proved unmovable.

Thus Plymouth, over the centuries, has developed in animated confusion and, as it reached the 1990's, had once more to look beyond its boundaries to house its people and give them work.

Its future as a regional capital is assured; its resilience is indisputable and its hopes are founded on sure and certain foundations.

—— COMPTON: ——
lush meadows and leafy lanes

Local historian R.N. Worth described Compton as the meeting of two shallow valleys which converged around a spur of higher ground at the head of a steep coombe, 'somewhat picturesque and shrouded in trees'. He would be surprised – perhaps shocked – to see its rapid development in the last seventy-five years, and not least at the garish blocks which loom over the ancient village beneath them. For all that, Compton Gifford is the last significant survivor of a village within a city, its atmosphere tranquil and balmy, an echo from a less jaded past.

No one seems to be quite sure where Compton Gifford itself actually begins and ends. The ancient tything included Higher and Lower Compton, nudging out to near Peverell. Still, the heart of the village is clustered around the Compton Inn, almost its oldest building, and to saunter around, taking in the high-walled lane adjacent to the pink Priory House, is akin to enjoying the atmosphere of a small village.

In spite of modern development, some of it rather stark and ugly, Compton Gifford retains its sense of difference, offering a little haven in the middle of a large city which has gobbled up everything around it.

In the early nineteenth century Compton – Higher and Lower – were very small villages inhabited almost exclusively by gardeners and small farmers. Plymouth people would enjoy an afternoon's stroll to the area to 'drink tea and eat fruit in the season.' To do so, they probably walked through Lipson and Mutley, also tiny villages in their own right. A contemporary historian records that they were 'much frequented in summer by the inhabitants of Plymouth to drink tea at.' Doubtless, farm labourers' wives made a little extra pin-money by serving tea in their front gardens or parlours.

In 1801, Compton Gifford had a population of only fifty, and all but five families worked on the farms or in the market gardens. Ten years later the hamlet had doubled in population, with some of the substantial houses built then standing to this day. The first of the remaining large houses, the Priory, now a residential home, had been built some time before 1800, thanks to a Captain Bremer, one of the several 'evacuees' from the once-fashionable Durnford Street area of Stonehouse.

The Compton Inn probably began its life in the early 1850s. At one time it contained a granary, tannery and a cobbler's shop, with its walls up to four inches thick in places. Captain Bremer gave the site, part of which was a pond, and £200 towards the cost of a small church, licensed in 1836; this was sufficient for the 270 people then living in the village. It marked the beginning of what was to become, in 1871, the Parish of Emmanuel, Compton Gifford. Planning for this had begun five years earlier when a private site was offered by Mrs Betsy Revel and her daughter,

Lower Compton set amid farms and orchards in this photograph from around 1900.

Elizabeth. Thus, by 1840, the village was beginning to enjoy a life of its own, with its own church, school and inn. In 1854, the experiment was tried of employing a paid constable at £52 a year and a Plymouth policeman, one William Horne, was appointed. The tide of inevitable change was lapping around the secluded little village, particularly with wealthy individuals from the Three Towns looking for somewhere to build themselves larger houses.

At the turn of the century market gardens and farms circled the village; a small stile beckoned walkers to the fields which separated them from Emmanuel Church. Four nurseries lay between Mannamead and Compton, one as far west as Hender's Corner — which became a terminus for the clopping horse trams. Market gardens were opposite the present post office (which retains its Compton Gifford motif over the door), stretching up to what now are the Co-operative Society playing fields.

A pathfield ran alongside the site of the off-licence at the bottom of the Blandford Road hill, with a stile which led to a smallholding which included ten cows. Cattle were run from Priory Farm, north of Priory House itself. On the brow of the hillock overlooking this lovely building is what looks like part of a ruined chapel but which, was a piggery near which a pony and trap were kept.

Mrs Sylvia Selly lives in one of the four villas in what is now Lower Compton Road. Built in the early 1800s, they were once known as Henrietta Villas, possibly as a delayed tribute to the wife of Charles I. Behind them are a set of six cottages built about 1730. They are almost invisible from the road but, grouped together with the

other villas, they help to preserve the village atmosphere. The long lush gardens convey an evocative charm. These houses used to have as neighbours nurseries and market gardens and smallholdings where poultry, pigs and goats were kept. Cows lazily chewed in fields on the far side of Compton Park Road. Mr Moses milked in a small shippon on the tip of Belle Acre Close, a site now occupied by an Exclusive Brethren meeting place. 'We used to keep our front gate shut to stop the cows from straying into our garden,' Mrs Selly recalls. 'Milk was delivered in urns, still warm from the cow.'

The rural character of the village and the fields beyond were vividly remembered by Mrs Lelah Williams. She was born in Beckham Place and lived in Compton all her life.

When I was a girl, Blandford Road was covered in fields and allotments, and cows used to lurch down the steep hill to what is now Grantley Gardens, Mannamead. You could reach Laira direct. There were fields at the end of the lane running alongside Priory House, and then a country pathfield which we called Castle Fields. Crowndale Avenue, off Chapel Way, was open country with a little stream running down the lane. At the top end pathfields ran to Eggbuckland Village, which was then miles out in the country and distinct in every way from Plymouth.

▲
Priory Road, Compton Gifford, taken from the east to west in the early years of the century. The small general shop on the left is now the village post office. It began life in 1910 with a Mr Turpin, an inspector at the tram depot. There have been two post-mistresses since those days.

▲

The pathfields to Eggbuckland village, from Compton Gifford, were used for direct access.

Compton, however, in spite of its rural character, was far from being a backwater. Mr Roy Hawke, the son of a successful local butcher, remembered the early days of two modern conveniences we now take for granted:

We were the first local family to go on to the phone, and that was back in 1909 when the whole system was still in a primitive state. We were also the first to own a car, ten years later. Not that we really needed it; trains were plentiful and cheap. The nearest station was at Lipson Halt, just a short walk away. The local 'puffer' began its journey at Marsh Mills, reaching the Millbay terminus via stations at Laira, Lipson, Mutley and North Road. From Millbay we could walk to Durnford Street, take a ferry to Cremyll and then walk on to Whitesand Bay without giving it a thought.

Mr Colin Blake was born at Carter's Place, opposite the present post office. His mother was only twelve months old when her family moved to the village in about 1870. Mr Blake remembered being part of 'a close-knit and warm hearted village community' in his boyhood.

My family had quite a stake in the village in that its one general store was run by my grandmother, Ann Ruse. This was opposite the Compton Inn and next door to a bootmakers, which my father owned. I used to help by taking weights and scales out to Roborough police station, there to be tested for their reliability, although sometimes my mother, Emily, would perform this chore herself, and walking all the way at that! When it was my turn I sometimes rode back to town in a Baskerville's horse tram.

A view of the old village before it started to spread, taken from near Compton Knoll House in the early 1900s. The fields in the background are now covered with part of the Efford estate. ◀

However, on leaving school at the age of fourteen, it was natural for him to turn to Plymouth to find work. There were also other changes afoot:

About this time a builder by the name of Charles Fox bought Priory House and erected a row of new houses along its spacious lawn; hence the new name of Priory Lawn Terrace. He named another terrace after himself and a third after his wife, Florence.

After leaving school I had to go to the Barbican each day to learn my trade as a shipwright. This meant catching a tram from nearby Mannamead Road, climbing over a stile and walking through fields to do so. I used to pass the island house now facing Blandford Road, backing onto Priory Road, then the only recognizable exit from Lower Compton to the great wide world beyond. I skirted a small farm adjoining what is now the built-up area of Compton Park Road.

The 'new road' in the early 1900s, but it has long been superseded. The white houses standing on their own used to be known as Henrietta Villas. ▼

'If I closed my eyes I could tell you who lived where in Compton more than seventy years ago' said Roy Hawke with that peculiar satisfaction of a man whose horse has come first. He was born in Carter's Terrace, opposite the present post office and his family roots went deep into the local community and his memories of the area are varied and fascinating.

Like for most of my generation, entertainment was mostly of the home-grown variety and entered into with great enthusiasm by the villagers. We used to have visits by one popular local group who called themselves the Compton Minstrels. They were a very versatile troupe who began life together in the little village school. They were so accomplished that invitations began pouring in for their services from all over the Plymouth area, and so fourteen men found themselves caught up in a social whirl that was entirely new to them.

The village has its share of characters, of course. I remember one, Captain Wright, who lived in an old cottage and who kept two monkeys which often clambered around an apple tree in the garden. We lads would throw stones at them and they would retaliate by picking off an apple and throwing it down on top of our heads.

Who would think that Compton Gifford once had a reputation as a kind of spa spot? This was thanks to a piped-off chute of water just a few yards up from what is now Crowndale Road. It was supposed to possess minerals which worked wonders for sore eyes and other ailments.

Granny Daw was the one for curing illnesses, though. She was a Romany gypsy from Beckham Place who lived to be more than a hundred and was greatly missed when she did die. Her reputation was proverbial and the villagers found her a constant source of help with a great variety of problems. Her boiled herbal treatments were supposed to cure carbuncles, boils and other skin annoyances. She even helped to deliver babies into the world and never lost one.

I went to see her once with a split lip. She told me to go home and ask my mother for a hairpin. Then I was told to take a little wax out of my ears and place it under my lip. I did so and was without a trace of it (the injured lip) the next morning. On another occasion my mother's foot was scalded when a dog rushed through the house and upset boiling fat onto it. It was that bad she couldn't get her boot on. Granny Daw arrived on the scene and asked for an old sheet. She took this down, put an iron on the stove, heated it and then singed the sheet. She then wrapped this around my mother's foot and within a week she could get her boot back on and her foot was completely healed.

—CATTEDOWN AND PRINCE ROCK:—
gateway to the world

The Cattedown area has been Plymouth's eastern 'workshop' for generations, the site of many of its heavier industries. Petroleum stores, chemical works, oil depots and smaller factories quickly filled the empty spaces left by extensive quarrying; it also has been the point from which the locally manufactured chemicals and fertilizers were dispatched. In addition, the bulk of the local china clay was sent to Cattedown to be shipped away, after arriving by rail from the moor.

The area has a link with a more romantic past, for it was from the Cattedown harbour that the great fleets of the medieval and Elizabethan eras set sail, including Drake's.

Cattedown has been run-down and generally unkempt for years but 1991 sees the beginning of its transformation when some 500 homes and attractive light industry is due to be provided under an urban aid programme.

Harry Chaffe, born and bred there, loves the place, and is always ready to recall the events and characters of bygone Cattedown.

It used to be a good place to be. Neighbours were friends and that friendship could be felt. My family roots were firmly embedded in the area; my maternal great-grandfather, Mr Thomas Hill, was a Barbican man who became a fish inspector. He and his wife, Lucy, lived in Southside Street where they raised their seven children. My grandmother, Marie worked as a 'skivvy' – her words! – at the old Royal Hotel. By the age of eleven she was pushing a milk cart around the Hoe for a local dairyman. She married my grandfather, Mr George Martin, a Coxside man who drove horses for Husham's, hauliers in Commercial Road.

He got a shilling a week for driving one horse and a guinea for driving two. He went on to be a Corporation dustman until an accident left him in poor health and without a pension. Lucy, my mother, worked in her mother's shop selling fish – cutlets of hake, 'pads' of queens, potted conger and mackerel, dressed crab and scallops.

It may have seemed very lucrative but people worked for a few coppers in those days. She was always dogged by ill-health and worked away until she was forced to stop. The shop was one of an amazing number in the area. Soaked fish, savoury duck, cooked pig's trotter and knuckles, udder and various other offal were all part of the shop scene.

For all that, traffic was so light that it was quite an event when anything arrived on wheels. The result was that you could play alleys or marbles, or use a whip and top, a hoop and even a grid – an old frame of a bicycle with two pram wheels

Cattewater and Laira Bridge.
◀

Boys playing on the beach at Queen Anne's Battery, now a superb yachting marina. Turnchapel village is on the other side of the river. To the left is the beginning of Cattewater. ▼

attached which you moved by pushing with your feet before coasting along. Then you had a vehicle handy for all sorts of things like racing or just running errands.

One game we played was extremely dangerous – running after lorries and jumping up to catch their tailboards and so cadge a ride. There was some accidents, I can tell you!

Of course, as the years slipped by so the traffic increased. In nearby Exeter Street, with its links to so many roads, this varied from massive steam engines pulling fair wagons to huge shire horses pulling timber and tree trunks to the Wicks and Hamblys yards. The horses left behind them droppings of much sought-after manure, scooped up quickly by local gardeners.

I can still remember the names of many of those local traders of sixty-five years and more ago … Exeter Street included names like J. Pengelly, saddler; J. Polkinghorne, butcher; Hender and Sons, leather merchants; H. Rockey, pies and pasties; R. Stribling, newsagents and C. Hesse, fruiterer. There were dozens more, of course, and all but a handful have disappeared.

It wasn't all work and no play, mind. Friary station was close and served as the departure point for jaunts into the country. It had an air of excitement, with the smell and hiss of steam, and with platform machines where you got a bar of Nestles chocolate for one penny.

Off we went to, say, Calstock for the day, picking some flowers to bring home, which I suppose seems rather quaint by today's standards. We spent the time at the other end playing with water pistols, being cowboys or Indians or just in games of one sort and another.

Still, such trips were few and far between and as adults our days were occupied mainly with hard work over long hours. Many varied cargoes were handled in Cattewater docks, the majority of them not seen there now. I remember there were potatoes from Ireland, cement, ore, timber, coal and

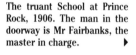

The truant School at Prince Rock, 1906. The man in the doorway is Mr Fairbanks, the master in charge. ▶

petrol. The Cattewater cooled the power station's vital parts. Ferries splashed energetically to Turnchapel and Creston, passengers often taking long looks at the early flying-boats then dotted around the water. Victoria Wharves, Coxside, was the departure point for steamers heading for Aberdeen, Bristol, Cardiff, Dublin, Dundee, Hull, Liverpool and other ports – quite a range when you think about it. It was a vibrant area playing an important role in Plymouth's economy which, later on, was allowed to run down.

Then, the workforce to sustain the stores and the landing of those cargoes meant a large number of dockers, most of whom lived in the area. It all helped to breed its own community feel, so different from anything there now. For instance, we had our own sports fraternity with local lads making names for themselves in the boxing world. Ted Moore, born in Prince Rock, was reckoned to be world class, and then we had the Murton brothers, Joe Symonds and 'Kelly the Kid'. The local football teams also drew large and enthusiastic followings – teams like Gashouse, Embankment United, Kittos, and many others. Now those players were the same men who worked so hard during the week, but they still played every match as if it was the FA Cup.

There were three local cinemas – the Palladium and the Cinedrome, in Ebrington Street, with the Plaza just further along. Some people preferred their entertainment at home, for the new radio sets were just coming along. Wires were everywhere in our houses, with an aerial stretching right across the room and out of the window, with the wires attached to the battery or accumulator. It was a work of art to find a station. On a 'big fight' night there was real tension. The set squealed, crackled and hissed until the magic voice of an announcer came through.

Another major diversion, although it happened only once a year, was Navy Days to which we invariably went, seeing such big capital ships as *Rodney, Furious, Renown* and *Royal Sovereign,* to name a few.

The old chemical works at Cattewater, long since gone, taken near Laira Bridge, with the limestone cliffs looming in the background. The site is now partially covered by the power station. ▼

This ancient hostelry stood on one of the oldest inn sites in Plymouth, dating from the fifteenth century. This one was demolished in 1902 to make way for modern premises. The Inn looked after the passengers for the Oreston ferry, and was a particularly welcome refuge on a cold winter's night.

It's easy to rhapsodize a bit mawkishly about the past, I suppose – as if everything was bright and beautiful, when it was far from being so. There were all kinds of seemingly petty inconveniences, like taking a bath, for instance. The houses were very small and bathing took place in a galvanized bath in front of an open fire. If there was a down-draught the smoke could make you blacker than when you started! Only canvas covered many floors, with distemper, often pink, on the walls. Often, an oil cloth covered the kitchen table, or else it was simply scrubbed clean. Boots were often 'tapped' in the kitchen with leather bought from local cobblers. Studs were hammered home to protect the soles, and the air could be blue if a thumb or finger got hit during this process.

Many of Harry Chaffe's experiences were echoed by Charlie Fice. The brawny ex-docker would clench his fists as he recalled the days when to 'work the ships' in Cattedown was synonymous with very long hours, poor pay and unbelievably hard conditions.

We were glad of the work, though. I've known what it is to be out of work for long periods with nothing coming in, and it wasn't funny. It was nothing to walk from my home in Emma Place, Stonehouse, to Oreston, Turnchapel and Cattedown to see if there was any work. I was just one man of many on similar errands, and I'd be home again by twenty past seven in the morning still without any. I even used to jump the railway bridge to avoid having to pay the ha'penny toll – that's how hard it was in those days.

It wasn't until 1925 I finally got work. It was just as well because that was the year I got married and I became a docker, an occupation I followed for the next forty years. My childhood and general background had fitted me for the rough, tough working life which lay ahead. I was actually born in Cattedown, at St John's Road, and left school early to become an errand boy for five shillings a week.

My strong political views began to evolve under the spell-binding oratory of the Sunday morning speakers who held forth at North Quay, Cattedown. They included George Ebury, who had a mane of long hair, and launched into passionate defences of the working man; he fought hard for the deprived of those days. He was one of several speakers who held 'locals' captive with their persuasive speeches, but at noon the pubs opened and they soon melted away.

My docking career was varied. I worked at steam trawlers which landed fish, and the many cargo ships which arrived at the Cattewater with machinery, timber, cement and manure. The whole area was very busy particularly in the years leading up to the First World War. We all worked hard. I thought nothing of carrying timber planks, 9 foot by 3 foot, on my shoulder, with the aid of a leather pad. And it was just an accepted part of the job to heave great bags of coal and potatoes about as well.

Sometimes my duties took me over to Millbay where I would go out in one of the tenders to meet the great liners which dropped anchor in the Sound, like the *Isle de France, Normandie,* the *Majestic* and, later, the *Queen Mary;* you could have eight a day call at peak summer periods.

The *Queen Mary* off the Eddystone Lighthouse. The great liners used to anchor in the Sound and were serviced by tenders from Millbay. One of Charlie Fice's jobs as a docker was to load and unload cargoes from these liners. ▼

My off-duty hours I spent in the Coxside and Cattedown districts, where I was born, brought up and lived for most of my married life. The local people were the most sporting in the world; they would always give to anyone who came around collecting for a good cause. There was a big sports following, too. I learned my football at Shapters Field, near Home Sweet Home Terrace, Cattedown, as most of us did. Crowds of up to 3000 used to watch 'local derbies' between such teams as Glanville United and Embankment.

Many Cattedown residents used the Barbican's shopping facilities, and I remember that these included Mary Readings' place and 'Mother' Nicholsons, two of the best pastry shops anywhere in the town. So much of all that has gone, now, and I missed Clare Buildings, where many of the dockers lived, and the friendly Clare Mission, run by the Congregationalists.

Some things I don't miss – like the way young children used to congregate outside the gas works at five o'clock to ask the workers if they had any spare bread or cakes; that was one side of Plymouth which many people didn't care to know about. On the other hand, fifty or sixty years ago you could leave your weekly rent on the window sill for the collector, and no one would dream of pinching it.

Skinning dogfish at the Barbican fish market. The Barbican was much frequented by the residents of nearby Coxside and Cattedown, for shopping, business and pleasure.
▼

Skinning Dogfish Barbican. Plymouth

—PLYMOUTH:—
the mother of them all

Mrs Ethel Rawlings recalled, at the age of ninety-five, the Plymouth of the early 1900s, as if she had just sauntered through its gas-lit streets the previous week. She was born in 1891, the year of the Great Blizzard, which her parents recounted to her in detail many times.

▲
Ethel Rawlings as a young woman. Her memories went back as far as the 1890s.

As everyone interested in the Great Blizzard knows, it paralysed the South West for weeks; sometimes stranded rail passengers huddled up to each other for twenty-four hours as they awaited rescue. My parents often talked about it and so did many other people in the years that I grew up in, before the turn of the century. It was quite a social ice-breaker, just as eye-witness accounts of Napoleon's appearance in Plymouth Sound had been eighty years earlier.

During the blizzard picks and shovels were used to clear the railway lines. My father, himself a railwayman, wore a pair of socks on his hands to keep them from freezing. When he came home and took his coat off it would stand upright on the floor because it was so frozen. One shop assistant reached the top of Grenville Road and was blown around a lamp-post, unable to move, until two men set her free and took her to her home in Desborough Road. People had to cling fiercely to the railings as they walked home.

My parents, called Fishlock, had moved to Plymouth from Dorset four years earlier, in 1887, when my father got a job as a porter at Friary Station. I went to the school at St John's, Coxside, at the age of three and was at once taught the alphabet and simple sums. Then I moved on to Cattedown Girls and Salisbury Road schools in due course.

I was eleven when the Boer War ended so I remember that quite well. I never forgot the sound of a middle-aged mother who used to walk up and down the back lane of the houses in Desborough Road crying – she had lost her son in that senseless war.

Of course, I can go back further than that, to 1897, when old Queen Victoria celebrated sixty years on the throne. I received a box of candies and a medal and I treasured both until they were swept into a rubbish bin by someone 'clearing up'.

We were given the presents at St John's Church, Cattedown, where we all went for a thanksgiving service. They were supplied by Tuckett's, in Millbay Road, I remember. In the evening Mother took us into the Guildhall Square to hear the band. When Edward VII was crowned in 1902 I received a bun in a bag from the

Opened in 1903, Salisbury Road School was used as a military hospital in the First World War and a billet for troops in the Second. Originally it had four classes; one for 'defective' and epileptic children, one for deaf children, one for pupil teacher instruction and the main school.

borough of Plymouth, and in the evening there was a huge bonfire on the Hoe, followed by music and dancing.

Mrs Emily Thomas, who was born in 1896, remembered the same event along with many others from her childhood.

One of my earliest memories is of a lovely tea-party at the school fields to commemorate the coronation of Edward VII and Queen Alexandra, in June, 1902. After speeches, patriotic songs and a very nice tea, every child was given a china mug and a medal.

Although my childhood was so happy, we were all conscious of many terrible and sad events. One which I remember clearly took place in June 1905, when the submarine *A8* went down in the Sound. The funeral of the victims took place with full naval honours, seven days later. Hundreds of people lined the streets at the funeral cortège wound its way to Ford Park Cemetery. None of us who witnessed that sad scene will ever forget it.

A few years along, I remember a solemn service at the Guildhall following the loss of the *Titanic,* in 1912. Many people were in tears because a number of Plymouth people went down with her.

The presence of a large Service population affected the texture of life in many ways.

Being a garrison town, Plymouth had a large number of soldiers too, and this affected many families. For instance, when a regiment left town families ran with it as far as they could, often to the docks where embarkation was made. Local people lined the streets when a regiment pulled out of say, Laira Fort for somewhere like India.

Badly bombed in the 'blitz', the Guildhall was saved from demolition by a single vote in the post-war city council. Opened in 1874, it became the venue for many conferences and concerts, as well as large scale services, such as that held for the victims of the *Titanic* in 1912.
◀

Funeral procession for the victims of the *A.8* submarine disaster. Fifteen men died when the boat sank outside Plymouth Breakwater on 8 June 1905. The cortège, seen here in Paradise Road, took an hour and a half to complete its journey, to Ford Park cemetery.
◀

Although the Navy always predominated in the city, many battalions of troops also were stationed here, particularly at Crownhill and Raglan Barracks. This boat is leaving Phoenix Wharf with locally-based soldiers for camp in May 1912.

All the Service population had to be catered for, entertainment-wise, apart from permanent residents. I remember the many celebrity concerts in the Guildhall with such world-famous singers as Dame Clara Butt and Madam Nellie Melba.

But, as Emily Thomas recalled, there was plenty of entertainment of a less elevated nature, although, perhaps exotic enough by today's standards.

We had Punch and Judy shows and barrel organs playing in the streets, with gaily-dressed monkeys trained to take pennies from the willing crowds. Dancing bears and German bands used to parade through the streets in the Edwardian 1900s. On Good Friday morning boys would go round the streets ringing handbells and selling hot-cross buns for a ha'penny each, or seven for tuppence. They were straight from the oven and, of course, tasted delicious.

There were also many organized events catering for the large population of the City. Very popular was the summer regatta.

Before and after the First World War there was something for everyone, really. People took the July regatta days as a kind of general holiday. They packed the Hoe and foreshore with thousands of spectators watching the rowing and sailing races, the swimming matches and the water polo. A fair with roundabouts and sideshows took place on the Promenade while ice-cream and fruit carts lined the Hoe from Tinside to Pebbleside. For all that, other events were popular too. We had tram races, tug-o'-wars between trawlermen, fancy dress parades with the boys taking part in 'bob apple' competitions and bun and treacle eating.

Smeaton Tower,
Plymouth Hoe

I am quite fascinated by
the "surroundings" here

In a naval town, souvenir cards with a nautical flavour abounded. However, the message reads: '... we cannot see much because it is simply pouring with rain.'
◀

▲
The old Theatre Royal, opened in 1813, sat approximately the same size audience as its modern namesake, 1192. It closed down in 1936 and, after demolition, the Corporation sold the site to a cinema combine.

All my generation loved the Pier, the starting place for so many trips by boat: up the River Yealm for a shilling, to Looe for four shillings and to the Eddystone Lighthouse for three shillings. It cost passengers one penny to go by steamer to Mount Batten or Turnchapel and Oreston.

Another great favourite was the old pannier market. Among the produce selling there eighty years ago were poultry, rabbits, fresh eggs, home-made butter, clotted cream, jams, hogs' pudding, home-made brawn and fresh garden vegetables. Farmers came from far and wide to sell their produce at the market, which was open until ten o' clock at night sometimes. When the food traders left at four o' clock their stalls were occupied by second-hand traders and that was the time the 'cheapjacks' turned up and provided an entertainment of their own.

On Saturday afternoons and evenings Plymouth's market drew particularly large crowds, attracted by the variety and colour of the stalls, and, as Mr Howard Spencer recalls, the wit of the stallholders.

People seemed to enjoy themselves even if they could not afford to buy anything – listening to the witty remarks of the stallholders, all of them shouting out about their goods. Some of the 'characters' who used to congregate there will still be remembered by the older generation.

There was Danny Cohen, with his pieces of jewellery and ability to repair watches on the spot; Phil Armstrong, who would be selling his favourite medicine with its secret recipe for body-building. He would take off his shirt and show the muscles of his arms and chest, claiming, of course, that they were the result of drinking his medicine. 'If you buy it and drink it, you, too, can have a body like mine!' he would shout.

Victoria Park is one of many sites in Plymouth based on reclaimed land. These Edwardian children are wearing the regulation bonnets, boots and serge stockings of the time.
◀

'Roll up and try one!' was the familiar invitation in the 1900s, when this picture of coconut shies at the West Hoe Park was taken.
◀

Boats out for the July Regatta in Sutton Harbour. ▶

'Make it a habit when you want a cup of tea, of calling at the café which overlooks the sea,' was the inviting suggestion which confronted visitors to the Pier, with its crumpled pleasure dome.
▼

An aerial view of the Pier and Tinside. The strange, banjo-shaped construction of the Pier was opened in 1884 and soon became the home for concert parties, home-made and semi-professional touring companies.

◀

Relaxing on the Hoe at the turn of the century. Smeaton's Tower and the Camera Obscura are clearly visible.

▼

Organized charabanc outings were all the rage in the 1920s. Destinations included Newton Abbot (for the races), Dartmouth and the main beaches of Cornwall – just like today. ▶

Markets have always been popular in Plymouth. This one, 'Tin Pan Alley', as everyone called it, was set up during the Second World War and remained for many years after, as this photograph from 1949 demonstrates. ▼

C.J. Park's the chemists, closed its distinctively old style shop on Mutley Plain in 1983, only to find itself carefully reconstructed in the Merchant's House as a museum. Its last owner, Mr Charles Armstrong Park, worked in the shop for sixty years. Here is his father and the staff, taken about 1910.
◀

The Chocolate Kid was another favourite character. He would take a large box of chocolates, place a slab of chocolate on top and one or two other items. Then he would start selling at about ten shillings, finally knocking the price down to half-a-crown or less.

Another great character of those times was Alf Spencer, known as the Linoleum King. He had two assistants, known as Slosher and Sausage. My job as a young lad was to hold the paraffin flare which used to light the stalls in the evenings, and for which I was paid a shilling a week.

With no supermarkets and pre-packaging, going shopping in the earlier years of the century was rather different to what we are used to now. Emily Thomas remembered the general stores, and the beginning of one of today's big names.

Service, and goods, in the shops was certainly different from today. The general stores, many of them quite small, sold everything from boots to lamp oil. Butter was placed in large slabs on the counter. The quantity asked for was measured off, weighed and formed into a pat. Then a pattern was imprinted on it; maybe a

J.N. Taylor's of Old Town
Street was typical of the
small ninenteenth-century
drapery shops scattered
around Plymouth's shopping
centre. This was one of
several similar shops duly
cleared to make way to provide larger premises for in-
coming firms. ▶

Drake Circus, the busy junc-
tion of Old Town Street and
Bedford Street. ▼

cow, swans or roses. Most general shops sported a huge pan at the door containing smoked dry cod or soaked green peas. Lard was sold from galvanized buckets. Every shop stocked a large jar of pickled onions, piccalilli and pickled cabbage on the counter. When Marks and Spencer first came to Plymouth they opened a penny bazaar in Cornwall Street, and the numerous things you could buy for a penny was quite amazing.

In the early years of the century, when horse-drawn traffic was common, the streets were no less busy than they are today. In fact this form of transport had its own hazards, as Emily Thomas recalled.

Horse-drawn trams were the main means of getting round the Plymouth of the early 1900s, and led to one terrifying occasion. Returning from Old Town Street to Mutley Plain, one of the two horses shied at a piece of paper blown by the wind. Passengers screamed as we were all jolted off our seats. It took the combined skill of the driver and his mate to pull them up at Townsend Hill. My mother refused to ride in a horse-drawn tram for many years after that.

Old Town Street was literally just that: the oldest street line of any consequence in early Plymouth. The street was remodelled in the late nineteenth century, only to be obliterated in the 'blitz'. Hand carts, horse-drawn vehicles and electric trams are all much in evidence in this picture from the early 1900s. ▼

The atmosphere of the streets, particularly before the era of electric street-lighting, is recalled by Emily Thomas with vivid affection.

Winter was the time when the lamplighter came into his own, armed with a long pole with a flickering light at the top to light the gas. When I was a child that seemed real magic. In the winter the postmen had little lanterns fastened to their uniform belts to enable them to see the addresses on the letters. There were six deliveries a day, mind you. Milk was delivered daily by a man with a horse and cart. The churns were covered in the summer with linens and, would you believe, the horses even wore straw hats with holes for their ears to poke through!

Side by side with these attractive aspects of a bygone era were frequent and unforgettable instances of poverty and hardship, as Emily Thomas remembers of the 1920s.

I don't intend to fantasize by making out that all the old days were full of undiluted well-being, because they weren't. I saw sights in Plymouth that would horrify people today. For instance, ragged and bare-footed children used to roam the streets. Drunken men and women fought each other and trouble between soldiers and sailors was common. After they had been quarrelling and fighting you would see them being frog-marched by the police to the cells behind the Guildhall. It could be very frightening.

Poverty was commonplace and many houses were badly overcrowded. The slums were dreadful places and yet, somehow, family life held together in a way that it doesn't do now. There was no dole money to help the unemployed, and there were many thousands of them in Plymouth then. One day a group of them marched to the workhouse in Wolseley Road to protest against the very unfair

Narrow cobbled streets, such as in this shot of Castle Steet in 1914, were once common in the old core of Plymouth. Only a very few examples survive, carefully preserved as showcases; they are no longer the crowded dwellings of the poor. ▶

Means Test. This demanded details about what money was coming in, how much furniture you owned, and so on. However, the march led to ugly scenes. The police were called and used their truncheons to restore order and disperse the mob of very angry men. That was before the General Strike of 1926 which produced yet more ugliness on the streets.

For those in work the hours tended to be long, and if you were young, the pay very low. However, for many young people, including Lily Facey, work provided an interest outside the home and opportunities for new experiences. Born in 1893, she left Johnston Terrace School in Keyham, to help bring up her brothers and sisters.

I was the eldest so I had to act as my mother's help, but I was probably more of a hindrance than anything! My first real job was as a waitress with Goodbody's in George Street and Bedford Street, at a wage of seven shillings a week. The hours were from half-past eight to five o' clock and I loved it. The owners, Mr and Mrs George Goodbody, were so thoughtful to all their staff, taking a personal interest. Many of the customers were among the better-off people, and some of them became good friends. The atmosphere was warm and congenial. And then there were those orchestras! We had them as a kind of background playing the popular tunes of the day while the customers ate toasted tea-cakes and 'fancies'.

Along with waitressing, another common kind of employment for young women was shop work. Ethel Rawlings entered the world of work this way.

At fourteen, it was time to go out into the world and earn my living. I was accepted as an apprentice draper with a Mr and Mrs Marchant, in St Judes. My world rapidly became one of haberdashery: ribbons, lace, millinery and cloth gaiters. By today's standards the hours were awful: nine in the morning to eight at night, with an extra hour on Friday evenings and staying at the counter until ten at night on Saturdays. But, truly, I loved the life. I was very happy.

Bedford Street was always considered the most up-market of Plymouth's shopping streets. It boasted fine stores in Dingle's, John Yeo's and, especially Popham's, favourite haunt of the well-heeled.

A later view of Bedford Street. The towering neo-gothic Prudential Assurance building was opened in 1904 and survived the blitz when everything round it was destroyed. Goodbody's Café, seen on the left, offered tea-time music from local bands, of which the Stan Wicks trio was among the most popular. ◀

Eliot Terrace was one of the finest buildings erected in the Victorian era. Number 5 was the home of Lord and Lady Astor for many years and now belongs to the city. ◀

WILL WHITEHEAD AND PAT GHILLYER:
these you have loved

A PREACHER'S LIFE

Will Whitehead's memories of Plymouth go right back to the Boer War. His life story is a remarkable one. Born in 1896, he became a Methodist preacher at the early age of seventeen and he remained active for most of his long life. He looks back on the variety of his preaching days with great warmth. Not all of his memories, however, are sweet. Of his childhood in particular, he remembers the daily battle to provide food for the table while his father was without work.

My parents were faced with a great struggle. Many a time I had to go to the butcher's shop and buy two pennyworth of bones for my mother to make soup, with the addition of groats, lentils and dumplings. Early mornings I would go to the baker's with a few pence to buy the stale bread that had been left over. I also went to Devonport Hospital to get a basin of dripping for a few coppers. With that, plus the bread and hot water, my mother made what we called 'kettle broth', and that was our breakfast. Those were indeed hard days, but we managed to survive.

We lived in Johnston Terrace, Keyham, and one of my earliest memories is the unveiling of the gun in Devonport Park in 1902 – it was a memorial of the Boer War, which ended that year. I knew about it all right because one of my uncles was killed in battle. Another early memory I have is waving to the great General William Booth, founder of the Salvation Army, as he drove down Albert Road in an open landau, his white beard whipped by the wind. That was in 1910, the year before he died.

I was often taken to the Brickfields to hear the splendidly-attired bands play on special anniversaries such as coronations, and other occasions. Many people listened to the band which played in Raglan Barracks Square every Sunday. I was in the crowd lining the streets of Devonport when the victims of the *A8* submarine disaster were buried.

Scenes like that, and many other smaller ones, have stayed etched on my mind all these years … poor lads, ill-clothed and without boots, begging for 'left-overs' from the lunch baskets of men working in the Dockyard … grown men singing on the streets for a few pennies, the favourite of the day being, strangely, 'Let your lower light be burning'. Of course, the old Three Towns were full of colourful characters, including Loppy Thomas and Billy Muggins who sang in the streets. One ditty Billy used to sing went:

I'm Billy Muggins, commonly known as Juggins,
Silly Billy, that's what my friends call me.
Why did the landlady call me her dear,
Treat me to drinks and to beer?
I'm Muggins, the Juggins
And Muggins I'll always be.'

Royal Albert Hospital, Devonport

The Royal Albert Hospital, where Will Whitehead bought cheap lard for his family. Built in 1863, it was for many years run on voluntary contributions. It was demolished in 1983 to make way for a block of flats.
◀

Johnston Terrace was one of a cluster of streets built in Keyham about 100 years ago. Johnston Terrace School was 'mixed' until 1930 when the boys took over the whole building; the name was changed to Tamar Central. The small general shop still stands.
◀

Occupying the site of old brickworks, the Brickfields has been a recreational and sporting area for over 100 years. It was the scene of many military parades, like this one in 1911. ▶

Union Street and the Octagon. The street was cut across former marshes in 1811 to give direct access to Stonehouse and Devonport from Plymouth. It soon became the favourite haunt of sailors on leave and acquired a notorious reputation. ▼

Woodbine cigarettes were five in a packet for a penny around 1906, and another song I've remembered all through the years is:

Five little fags in a dainty little packet,
Five cigarettes that cost one D.
Five little whiffs – and in five little tiffs
He was lying on the tramway line
Wishing he could touch the cable,
Looking greener than the label,
Oh, his little Willie Wild Woodbine!

When we lived in Albert Road I became familiar with horse-drawn buses which travelled to the Octagon in Union Street. I used to nip on one to take me to St James's Hall for the early silent pictures, on such subjects as the Russian-Japanese war. We moved to Alexandra Road, Ford, which gives me a memory of a very different kind with a Mr Rowe, a Methodist local preacher from Honicknowle, who would come by with his little cart, drawn slowly by six donkeys.

We moved again, this time to Morice Square, when I started attending the Naval and Military School at the rear of King Street. From there I could watch horses being brought over on the Torpoint Ferry, bound for hard labour in the Dockyard, poor things. The old Navy training ship, the *Impregnable,* lay just off Mutton Cove, nearby, and I often went aboard to see my brother, Albert, who received his early training there.

While still at school, I started to help out at Ware's ironmongers' shop from eight o' clock for forty minutes before going off to school, and report back there

▲
Horse traffic in Union Street. The first official system of horse tramways in Devonport and Plymouth started in 1879. On the left can be seen the entrance to the Grand Theatre.

The *Impregnable* training ship was one of the old 'wooden walls' battleships built in the early 1800s. Its three decks could accommodate 200 men who often slept, worked and trained in its confined quarters. ▶

from half-past twelve to a quarter-past one, in case they wanted any errands run. I was back again after tea for an hour and all day Saturdays, and my wage was just two shillings and sixpence!

When I left school I was apprenticed to a blacksmith in Plymouth. I left home in Ford at six o' clock in the morning and walked into Plymouth, and I loved the work. Later, I managed to get an apprenticeship with the Co-operative Society, at a weekly wage of four shillings, and I went on to serve with them for nearly fifty years, finishing up as branch manager of the grocery and provision shop on Mutley Plain.

Of course, that whole area of Ford, and Devonport, has changed tremendously over the years; it's hard to think I used to play football over what is now St Levans Road, or that I used to pick watercress – and fresh at that – from the stream flowing at Weston Mill.

One thing that hasn't changed a bit, though is my love of preaching, and I was a Methodist Local Preacher for over seventy-two years, which is quite a record. Perhaps I shouldn't say it but by the age of seventeen I was advertised at the Morice Town Salvation Army Hall, in Gloucester Street, as 'the boy preacher'. When I returned home from army service after the First World War I settled at the Old Herbert Street Methodist Church, and the urge to preach grew ever stronger.

At home was a large volume of what was called *The Home Preacher,* in which were sermons from the great preachers of the day and recent past, such as Charles Haddon Spurgeon and Dr Witt Talmage. I used to place this volume on a chair which, to my young mind, was my pulpit. Around the room I would place other chairs in a circular position – and there was my imaginary congregation. Then I would read the Scriptures, sing hymns and read one of the sermons, playing at preaching was one of the highlights of my younger days.

The transformation from playing to the real thing began in 1912 when I was asked, one Sunday, how I would like to become a preacher! It was just what I had been waiting for. 'I'd love to preach', I replied, without a moment's hesitation. And that was the start of my life's love. I was accepted on to the Plan in 1913 and, eventually, my preaching took me all over the West Country and even beyond.

In those days we local preachers had to make long journeys. Sometimes it meant my walking ten miles to the church and then ten back home again, and that at night. To arrive at some chapels in time for the morning service meant leaving home at seven in the morning, after being at work the previous day from eight in the morning to ten at night, and no matter what the weather was like.

As I look back over so many years of preaching, I ask, 'Has it been worth it?' My answer is 'Yes', for there have been compensations that have rejoiced my heart and sent me singing on my way.

BEHIND THE SILVER SCREEN

Pat Ghillyer probably knows more about the old silent films and the advent of 'talkies' than anyone else in the West Country and when he talks about them he starts to 'rewind' an invisible reel. The cinema, he says, has been his one and only love; he started working in them at Devonport over sixty-five years ago, when he was a lad of twelve. He was born in Cornwall Street and remains a Devonport devotee.

Many of the early 'picture houses' were converted shops or garages, and this included one of Devonport's favourites – the Tivoli, in Fore Street. This site had been occupied by Allens' auction rooms until 1909, when it was taken over by Mr Harry Frost who transformed them into a 350-seater cinema. The seats were not of the most luxurious – six rows of benches immediately in front of the screen, followed by ten rows of wooden tip-ups and then more of the same. In those early days the usherettes, most of them elderly, made cups of tea for patrons during the matinées, which ended at four in the afternoon.

Then, in due course, a new manager arrived who was to stamp his image not only on the Tivoli but also the town, and in a vivid way at that. Mr Harry Harcourt was a born showman and he soon began to attract a large following. Quite an entertainer in his own right, he could sing and tap-dance, tell comic jokes and

The Tivoli and staff, 1937. Pat Ghillyer (second from the right), then chief projectionist, is standing beside the manager, Mr Osborne.

generally patter away. He would often make two appearances during the programme, on the small stage in front of the screen, and to the huge delight of the packed audiences.

Business really started booming after the First World War with many families regarding the Tivoli as a kind of second home. I remember enjoying the Saturday matinées as a child. The first 100 children in were given comics, such as the *Rainbow*, and at Christmas we were given fruit. Harry Harcourt certainly knew how to draw his audiences and hold them together as one happy family. I started running messages for him when I was twelve and I was allowed to remain at the cinema until nine in the evening. There's no doubt I was bitten by the film 'bug' right from the start and soon knew that I wanted to become an operator; they never called us by the fancy name of projectionist in those days.

I had to go up into the box and learn how to rewind the nitrate films. At other times I would stand at the back of the operating box and stare in awe and fascination at the projectors. I learned all the aspects of running a cinema the hard way. That included billposting, changing the outside 'stills' and damaged seats, unchoking the toilet pans, scrubbing the wooden floor beneath the seats and delivering posters – all that, and I loved the life!

Harry Harcourt was dubbed the patron saint of Devonport when he let those who were unemployed come in for 1½d, until four o' clock. During the Tivoli's

The Forum was one of three cinemas in the old Fore Street. Opened in 1938, it survived the 'blitz', but falling attendances forced the first of several changes in 1961 when it was turned into an indoor sports arena. Now it is a Bingo hall. I remember my mother taking me to a film there soon after it had opened.
◀

silent film days, a pianist, a cellist and a violinist played appropriate music. In 1926, when the 'Tiv' put on the Conan Doyle epic, *The Lost World* for a week, the Dockyardies came rushing out of the Fore Street gate at five o' clock and went straight into the queue, to catch the middle performance.

In later years, Mr Harcourt was elected to the management of the old Royal Albert Hospital. He used to dress up as a circus clown during the town's annual carnival week until his sudden death, in 1934. Eventually, I became chief operator under the new manager, a Mr Osborne. But when the new Forum opened in 1938 just down the road, but on the opposite side, it spelt doom for the 'Tiv' which was forced to close not long after.

The nearby Electric cinema was housed in Devonport's former public hall, which later became the YMCA building. This opened in 1910. The projection box was erected on stilts at the High Street end of the old building, with the new square screen at the Devonport Park end. The ground floor seated about 500 people. A balcony ran along the right side of the building, presumably used by members of the public to follow debates in the days when it was a public hall. Patrons had to pay 2d for a seat up there, but the funny thing was they all had to turn their heads to the right to see the picture! This meant that those sitting in front of the balcony near the screen experienced the weird prospect of elongated shadows on the screen. It was a pretty hopeless situation, so, after the first showing, they were all allowed to stay behind for the second house, moving back as a sort of compensation!

In 1931 the whole of the building was raked and from it arose a beautiful new 'super' Electric with 2000 seats; all was luxury and comfort. The first film, in 1932, was *Trader John.* On opening day the Lord Mayor, Alderman Clifford Tozer, made a befitting speech from the stage, with an army band in attendance. The very first magnascopic screen, the forerunner of the Cinemascope, was installed and, when fully expanded, the screen filled nearly all the stage. A special 'cat's eye' lens was fitted on the projector for this and it moved and increased the focus as the screen was expanded. Alas, the Electric was a casualty of the 1941 bombing: one of many cinemas to be destroyed all over Plymouth.

The 'Electric' can be seen just by the tram at the top of the picture. Before 1910 it had been a public hall. It had a large stone wall screen on the Devonport Park side; patrons in the gallery on the Fore Street side had to swivel their eyes right in order to even see the screen! ▼

Many Devonport people were also devotees of the Hippodrome Theatre, built in 1902 and enjoying many first-run shows from London. It was basically a variety theatre but it switched to films in 1930 and had to be altered slightly for a projection box to be built on the roof. The new-style 'Hipp' opened with a blaze of publicity, screening the feature musical film *The Broadway Melody.* This, too, was bombed to the ground during the blitz. By then, though, many great names had appeared there, including Gracie Fields, George Robey, Florrie Ford and Gertie Gitana.

The Hippodrome, in Prince's Street, was opened as a music hall in 1908, and boasted 2000 seats. Later, like most of its contemporaries, it turned over to films and was destroyed by bombs in 1941.
◀

The other theatre in Devonport was the Alhambra, in Tavistock Street, first known as the Empire and then the Metropole. Opened in 1924, it didn't really enjoy a good reputation as a stage theatre and its most successful productions were vaudeville. The Alhambra also tried its hand with 'movies'. It was wired in 1929 by an American firm, However, first-run films at both the Electric and the Hippodrome proved far too much in the way of opposition, and trade fell off. It closed in 1932, but not for long; just six months later it made another effort to recapture its former audiences and managed with such superb shows as Tommy Handley with his hilarious series of sketches called 'The Disorderly Room'. Little did any of us guess that this comedian was going to do so much to boost a whole nation's morale in the coming war. Unfortunately, German bombs destroyed this fine old theatre as well.

The Tivoli's male staff had to stay all night once a year to change the screen, a job which could take up to five hours. Screens used to get very stained with cigarette and pipe smoke, the dirt clogging up thousands of tiny holes. The black masking around the proscenium had to be undone and white tapes threaded through dozens of large brass eyelets.

All cinemas had their doormen, or commissionaires; the Tivoli's was a splendidly-built ex-Serviceman who sported a big beard and wore his medals proudly on his resplendent uniform. Both he and Mr Harcourt would stand out front-of-house each afternoon and evening calling out: 'All seats guaranteed at sixpence and a shilling!' Four rows of red plush seats were installed at the back of the cinema – these were the shilling ones; the others were priced at 3d, 6d and 9d.

—PLYMPTON:—
the first among equals

Less than sixty years ago Plympton was surrounded by lush meadows and marsh land, with Woodford a country 'buffer' on the way to Plymouth. The village was the centre of a vital community life, patronized by the landed gentry who lived in beautiful country houses on land later to be gobbled up by the house builders.

Any true Plymptonian will tell you that three into one won't go; that Plympton St Mary, St Maurice and Underwood have different characteristics not yet submerged under the bland blanket of 'identi-kit' invasion from the west. For years, the hub of Plympton was the Ridgeway, that long Roman road which has seen the march of legions, of English kings on their way to war with France and of retreating Cavalier forces in the Civil War.

For hundreds of years Plympton was deep in the heart of the country, with the white-foamed Tory Brook serving as a reminder that the clay workings weren't far away. This is the setting in which the Pearse family farmed in the nineteenth century. Walter Pearse, an extraordinarily articulate man, remembered how his father, John, used to sell sheep in Stone Barton before he founded the well-known firm of agricultural auctioneers which bears his name.

Yes, his voice became familiar in the markets of the South Hams, particularly at Modbury, Yealmpton and Plympton itself, even after he had passed eighty. He could be heard calling the bids over the clamour of lowing cattle. He farmed extensively at Chaddlewood, now engulfed by urban sprawl. The family also farmed at Torridge Way, little guessing that so many farms were to be swept away by house-building.

This began at Woodford between the two world wars and was accelerated by Tecalemit's arrival at Marsh Mills. It wasn't long before they were building on land used as market gardens, let alone the good agricultural land at Yealmpstone years 'later. The land had been farmed for hundreds of years; my family was farming locally in 1803.

I grew up in the old St Mary's vicarage at the bottom of the Ridgeway, not far from Dark Street Lane, and which is still standing. My brother, Frank, and I joined an auctioneers business founded by my father and I sold 800 South Devon bullocks in one day at the Plympton market in the old days.

The market's origins were at Longcause, St Maurice; my father sold cattle at the sale ring by the gate of what is now St Peter's Home but as traffic built up the police objected to the sales in the middle of the street. So the auctioneers walked across the pathfields to sell sheep at Scoble's Field, near St Mary's church, and it moved to its present site in 1909.

▲
The Ridgeway, around 1900, taken from Dorsmouth Rock. The straggly line in the immediate foreground is Underwood village, with Saltram Terrace, Plympton St Mary, beyond it.

St Elizabeth's House, at the top of the Ridgeway, when it was run by the Sisters of Mercy as an old people's home. ▶

The family largely ran the Yealmpton Show for fifty years and in the days, at that, when many titled people attended. People would come to it in horses and traps, although we used a brougham. I think patrons went to the show to meet each other as much as anything. Everyone knew everyone else; it was a great social occasion. People would hop into our trap for a chat and we would do likewise; folk had much more time for each other then.

The rural character of Plympton in the early part of the century is remembered fondly by those who spent their childhood there. Joan Gullett recalls its setting:

The Ridgeway was the hub of Plympton; then very much a self-contained village. There were houses either side, and along Moorland Road too, but beyond that we had lovely green fields and small woods; we were really in the country and we loved it. Woodford, further along on the west towards Plymouth, was a mass of fields and marshlands. The boundary was at Longbridge and children called the Tory Brook the 'Whitewash' because that's the colour it was as it carried china clay ...

Biddie Goad had vivid memories of the local dairies:

St Maurice was a tiny village eighty years ago, mostly grouped around Fore Street, which had fourteen shops, and I can remember most of them quite easily. Three sisters ran a dairy by the name of Scobells, and you could eat off their floor, it was that clean. They used to measure their cream with pebbles on the scales, and they would shine like pieces of gold. You could buy two-pennyworth of cream. New cream was twopence and scalded one penny a pint.

Two dairies were opposite Miss Scobells': Hicks' and Watts'. Another one was down the road called Stephens' and Miss Vosper had hers near the church. She had china swans in her windows, filled with eggs. I used to carry milk for her in the morning which meant getting up at 6.30 and the job took well over an hour. I returned home for breakfast and then it was off to school.

Mrs Goad's family lived in Caroline Place, on Fore Street. She moved here when she was only eight months old. Her grandfather was an important local person: he was both the water bailiff and the captain of the fire brigade. One of Mrs Goad's earliest memories is of the old malt house, just off the main street and now a nursing home for old people. It was used primarily to dry hops for beer, but local people found other, more informal, uses for it, such as bringing clothes there to dry overnight.

It cost one penny a basket and one man was always on duty there overnight to keep an eye on the clothes. Ivy, my sister, used to help me carry the basket. In the morning we would go back and the clothes would be dry.

The separate parts of Plympton enjoyed their own strong sense of neighbourliness. For the newly married Edie Gale, Colebrook provided all the security she needed:

I married in 1914, my husband working at 'Treverbyn' in service with a Mr Martin, who was the equivalent of an executive with the English China Clay Company. We lived at Colebrook in a little row of cottages for seven years and those were the days of street outings, when all the neighbours knew each other well. It was all so different! Why, you could leave the doors of your house wide open and most of us did. Neighbours would pop in and out to see you and if you were ill there was no shortage of help.

The different communities that made up Plympton were themselves remarkably self-contained and certainly in the eyes of their inhabitants, possessed very different

▲
The Old Ring 'O Bells public
house in Underwood, about
1900. It was demolished in
1937, but the rest of the
buildings are little changed
from this scene.

The 4ft 6in. gauge line ran
near Plympton from the Lee
Moor china clay pits to Coxside. Many clay workers lived
in the Plympton area.   ▶

▲
The west end of Underwood
Road, with the Saltram estate
to the left and Underline to
the right.

characters. The young Joan Gullet found her surroundings at St Mary adequate for most of her needs:

Normally we had no cause to go over to St Maurice or Colebrook, although we did go to the latter for ironmongers' and general stores. A walk around the pathfields was all that drew us to St Maurice.

Cheek-by-jowl with St Maurice was the old village of Underwood, considered the less salubrious of the two communities. Frank Sluman, born in St Judes, moved there with his family in 1920. 'Frankly, Underwood was something of a dead and alive hole in those days. It was St Maurice which had a touch of class; people who had 'anything' lived there.' He found it a typical working-class area, peopled mainly with farm and clay workers, most of them ex-Navy.

In those days they used to bring clay down the line from Lee Moor after loading it by hand. Some of the men were taken with clay-worker's disease so badly that they could hardly breathe. Many died young, but the paradox was that many lived to a ripe old age.

Many of the houses in Underwood were small, a few almost derelict. One room downstairs and two up, or the other way round, was common, although there were larger dwellings including Bellevue Dairy, owned by Mr Bob Giles. Toilets were mostly outside and few boasted bathrooms.

Still, the little community did sport colourful characters. Joe Morton could paper a room and paint its ceiling in ninety minutes flat and still come out of it ready for more. Alf Pope kept stables opposite Bellevue Dairy, but he did a neat line in vegetables as well. He would put a green coloured sheet over his wagon

and sell vegetables in the district. People used to try to watch what he was doing in his store-cum-stable, and some deduced that he was counting onions!

Further down the road was the Gilbert family; the oldest son, George, did a vegetable round by pony and trap. They had a daughter, Rose. She married a naval pensioner when she, too, was getting on in years but still managed to bear him five children.

Soon after we moved to Underwood I was taught to play the violin by Bill Roberts, up at St Maurice. For some reason the sight of me walking down the street with a large violin case under my arm was a ceaseless cause of merriment.

The young, whatever community they were tied to, had one basic thing in common: entertainment was mostly of the home-grown variety, as Edie Gale of St Maurice recalled:

Artificial entertainment was sparse by today's standards. There was a small cinema at the bottom of Station Road but practically nothing else to do in the village apart from periodic dances in the George Hotel. Against this background, though, you had to set far more in the way of family life. All of us did more together, including the playing of simple games.

There were organized entertainments, though, and some were traditional celebrations on a large scale. Biddie Goad remembered several:

PLYMPTON BAND OF HOPE DEMONSTRATION

One of the great annual events was the May Day celebrations at the Castle when coloured ribbons would flutter on the large maypole, to be danced around by the children of the neighbourhood. It was a wonderful outing which always finished with a good tea. Other events took place, too, on the Castle Green, including circuses, travelling zoos and other attractions. We would play hoop-la there, and swings and roundabouts were provided.

The following event, described by Joan Gullet, must have been particularly popular:

One of the great Plymptonian institutions was the Good Friday hot cross bun 'scramble'. People from miles around got up as early as five o'clock to wait outside Perraton's shop in the Ridgeway to buy their buns, the recipe for which was a closely-guarded secret. Festivities went on for hours, including dancing in the streets, much music and a little touch of discreet courting.

Eagerly looked forward to were the outings, special events in the days before the motor car revolution. Biddie Goad remembered the excitement and the enjoyment:

Plymouth was very definitely another place; we went there for work or summer outings, but hardly at all otherwise. Wembury was a popular choice for outings, I remember. Mr Hicks would take us in an old coal cart led by horses. We thought that a marvellous outing.

The annual Band of Hope demonstration, parading down Market Road in 1910. The Hele Arms is in the background.

PLYMPTON HOUSE

St Peter's House, one of the several country houses in the area, was built in 1720 for the Treby family. It was once known as the Great House or Plympton House and is now a convent.

The large country houses of the 'gentry' and the families that lived in them had an important influence on the community. Walter Pearse remembers the details:

Plympton still sported a clutch of country houses in the 1920s, all occupied by families of note. Harewood House was owned by Captain Tolcher; General Mudge and his family lived in Sydney House, Dark Street Lane. Colonel Solteau-Symonds was in residence at Chaddlewood House, surrounded by woodlands and fields. Hillside was the home of the solicitor, Cecil Hewes, who built a local school. He favoured the 'there are no losers in life' policy and did something practical about it by giving a prize to every one of the eighty school pupils.

Frank Sluman who worked as a carpenter in the area, remembered the fate of Sydney House:

I helped in the construction of the Plympton Pentecostal Church which stands on the site of General Mudge's home …in Dark Street Lane. He was one of the finest men in this country let alone Devon. Unfortunately the house eventually was left derelict as he died without family.

This lovely lake, set in the grounds of Chaddlewood House, was long ago swallowed up for building sites. The house itself was built in 1883 for the Soltau-Simons family and has been restored. Detachments from the Indian Cavalry were billeted here during both world wars.

◀

WESTON MILL, NORTH PROSPECT AND
—ST BUDEAUX:—
the old north-west frontier

The waters of Weston Mill Creek used to flow right up to the edge of the ancient hamlet with barges sailing to unload corn. This was ground at the old water mill which worked busily until the 1890s. Timber was floated up from Bere Alston; a narrow lane on the outskirts of the village served as the main route between Plymouth and Saltash, connected by a ferry. Years later an enormous reclamation project dissipated the Creek. However, in spite of the many changes all around the area, including the great snake-like swathe of the St Budeaux by-pass, the heart of the village remains very much what it has been for centuries.

Of the 'mill', a survival can be found in the shape of one of the two huge mill wheels, still preserved in Mrs Winifred Glass's house; the axle of the other is outside in the garden.

Her association with the area began when she worked for Lord Trelawny-Ross at nearby Ham House as an 'in between' maid, and it is there that she met her husband, Arthur. He was a farmer on the Ham estate, whose forebears had lived in Weston Mill for generations. Her mother-in-law told her of the days when timber was floated up the village stream from Bere Alston, having been brought most of the way by boat. 'She, and her father before her, used to grind the corn that arrived here.'

Mr Eddie Prowse and his family moved to Weston Mill ninety years ago, when, he says, it was 'just like living in the country.'

In those days the Creek lapped its way over Camel's Head and what are now the playing fields fronting Ferndale Road, to the very edge of the old village itself. Fellows used to fish from the bank where the sewage works stand, and my father remembered the barges gliding up to the village loaded with grain. It certainly was very much a country life. For instance, if I wanted a rural walk in the early 1900s, I had a variety of choice in the leafy lanes which eventually led into Plymouth. In those days it was country all the way to Pennycomequick and we walked between hedges, past fields and farms. In fact, it was all fields and farms at Churchway and most of St Budeaux and Honicknowle. Stables used to straddle the land near what is now Wolseley Road. One, owned by a Mr Cleave, looked after thirty horses all of which worked in Devonport Dockyard. Cattle used to graze over the rising slopes surrounding Weston Mill.

Later, of course, the railways came, with the old London and South Western line running parallel to Ferndale Road, with halts at Weston Mill itself and Camel's Head. I remember that services included 'hops' to such places as Okehampton, Exeter and Callington. In those days. though, everyone walked a

▲
The bridge at the heart of the
ancient hamlet of Weston
Mill, as it looked in the
1880s.

◄
The rural setting of St
Budeaux in the early 1920s,
with the Trelawney Hotel
(centre foreground) at the
hub of the village. Houses
now cover all the fields. The
houses near the skyline were
part of the King's Tamerton
area.

great deal more than they do now. For instance, my maternal grandfather walked to the Dockyard from Tamerton Foliot, and back again, a total distance of about eight miles. Incidentally, his pay was only eighteen shillings a week, but he brought up three sons and eight daughters on it.

I went to school at Johnston Primary, in nearby Keyham, where discipline was strict and the teacher's word was absolute law. A cane hung in the corner of every classroom and it wasn't for decoration. I remember that a few of us lads cut sacks of potatoes on a farmer's cart so that they all rolled down a hill. The farmer turned up at school on a sort of identification parade, soon picking out the culprits. Each of us received eight strokes of the cane on the arms – both of them. It hurt all right, but it taught you to behave yourself.

I was one of nine children, six of them girls, and I remember my mother walking all the way into the centre of Plymouth to sell flowers outside the main entrance of the Continental Hotel, something she had been doing since the age of twelve.

Ham House was built for the Trelawney family in 1639 who owned it until it was sold to Plymouth City Council in 1947. In the early years of this century the estate was a favoured poaching ground and vigilantly patrolled by gamekeepers.
▼

The rural character of Weston Mill in the early years of this century is vividly recalled by Mr James Pope. His verdict on the place is simple and spontaneous: 'it was absolutely lovely!'

There were the nearby Ham Woods, but these were closed to the public, being the strictly private preserve of Lord Trelawny-Ross who, in his horse-drawn carriage, was a familiar sight to local people. The woods were full of pheasants – I bagged a few myself, mind. But His Lordship employed three men to keep his

woods clear of intruders. The village was surrounded by farms on three sides, many of them producing masses of juicy fruit. Apart from Bill Bennett, the other farmers I can remember were Sam Middleton, the Martin brothers and a Mr Treeby, all of them into fruit, growing plums, apples and strawberries. There was a large pond at the bottom of the village, and tramps used to come to drink from it. Freshwater trout jumped through the stream which came in from Camel's Head.

Opposite what is now the tip was Butlin's Farm with a big orchard over the hill, perched on top where the water authority's buildings now stand. Higher still was Mr Deacon, a blacksmith. We only had one general shop – it was all we needed. It sold just about everything including postage stamps and was run by Mrs Evans, followed by Mr Leeman. One way and another we spent a lot of time in the fields or the woods; the farms themselves stretched all the way from Weston Mill to Honicknowle, which was then another village on its own. I remember the toll-gate at the end of the little bridge which still spans the village. Mrs Hatherleigh, a member of a well-known Weston Mill family, used to live in the toll-house.

In my father's time the toll-gate was important because it stood astride what was then one of the main roads to London. Horses pulling wagons would come down, their due would be paid and, at the top of the hill at St Budeaux, they would be changed for two fresh animals. We really felt we were out in the country in those days; goodness, a trip into Plymouth was something to be talked about for the rest of the week! We used to stroll across the fields to Camel's Head, where the tip is now, and for a penny ha'penny could ride into the town centre, and if you caught the tram at Milehouse instead it only set you back a penny.

St Budeaux was also very much a rural area with large fields covering what is now Pemros Road, leading to the Tamar railway bridge. I remember that there were five different stables and we used to go along to the annual horse show which was a major event. Moor Lane, and all around it, was a country lane and several farms stretched to Bull Point. I started work at fifteen on one of them with Bill Bennett who had fifteen acres and part of Coombe Farm as well.

St Budeaux Terrace, St Budeaux. Many older residents have seen St Budeaux grow from a self-contained village to a large and noisy suburb. Its name comes from St Budoc, the Breton Saint, who arrived at Tamerton Creek in A.D. 480 and introduced Christianity to the area.
◀

THE SQUARE, ST BUDEAUX.   3188

That was the beginning of over fifty years of an open-air life of one sort and another. I helped to pick strawberries, of which there was a profusion, starting at seven in the morning, with an hour for lunch and knocking off at about five-thirty, all for twenty-eight shillings a week. Mind, those were the days when if you couldn't work you didn't get paid. Rain was bad news for farm workers so we went on until we nearly drowned!

In later years, after a spell as a gravedigger at Weston Mill cemetery, among other things, I started up on my own as a fish salesman. I would go down to the Barbican, bid for fish and then retail it to the Camel's Head area, St Budeaux and Weston Mill. It was a hard living, no doubt about that, but I did it for seven years and I didn't finally retire until I was seventy. I was driving tractors then for the Ministry of Defence at its Ernesettle depot and they practically had to order me to go into retirement! I've never been afraid of hard work, I have loved doing so much of it in the open-air and there is no place in the world I would sooner have lived than Weston Mill. To me it is still a village on its own and always will be, never mind what the planners do all around us.

A MUNICIPAL MARVEL:
the Swilly Estate

Seventy years ago overcrowding in Plymouth centre was almost the worst in England with 200 people living per acre — worse by far, than the situation in London's East End or in Liverpool. Only 2500 municipal houses had been built by 1920, a meagre figure indeed. But then Lord St Levan offered to sell some of his land to the Corporation and so the Swilly estate (now back to its original name of North Prospect) was born. Hundreds of houses were built on the 178 acres that were made available.

Swilly houses were of two types, known officially as parlour and non-parlour. The first had an extra room downstairs and that put another shilling on the rent and rates, which totalled about twelve shillings a week. This figure did not rise much until the

Second World War. By this time some tenants had decided to return to the older parts of the City simply because they missed their friends and the local life they had left behind.

Lord St Levan, had the foresight to insist that certain old trees were to remain as a feature of the lay-out, fortunately for future generations. So, remain they did, and many still are there today. One of the main attractions for Swilly tenants was that each house had a reasonably sized front and a rear garden with privet hedge boundaries. One of Lord St Levan's former trees stood outside every dwelling on a grass border and a macadam pavement, a rare luxury indeed in a city more overcrowded than most.

Such features might not attract much attention today, but according to Mr Norman Bargery, whose parents were among the first people to move into the estate, they were a great leap forward in the 1920s.

This was especially so compared with the cramped, closed-in dwellings that some of the early inhabitants had left behind. The builders provided several large open spaces, something unknown in the older housing areas. In every way, then, Swilly was a great improvement. For instance, a little copse, a field and a stream were left as a feature between Knowle Avenue and North Down Crescent, which were the first roads to be constructed. Everyone greatly appreciated this simply because there was beauty and a lovely playground right by the houses, with some trees and shrubs in an adjoining field, some of them still there today.

An early aerial shot of the North Prospect estate. The old workhouse is at the bottom of the picture. The relative spaciousness of the sixty-five-year-old estate can be contrasted with the older, cramped terraces of Ford, on the bottom left-hand side.

Apart from anything else, they provided us young lads with blackberries and birds' nests.

Before long, Swilly extended to the North Prospect area with the eventual addition of Cookworthy Crescent, Grassendale Avenue, Beacon Park Road and other streets. A school was built near Swilly Road but most children still went to Johnston Terrace Junior School, Camel's Head, with a few attending the Roman Catholic School in Renown Street, Keyham.

A field of about 300 acres between Royal Navy Avenue and North Down Crescent provided two football pitches, as well as tennis courts, and two local teams played there, St Thomas and Keyham Athletic. At that time the hero of Plymouth Argyle was their goalkeeper, Harry Craig. Many a young lad playing in goal on the Swilly pitches hurled himself around in what he thought was Craig's style!

Swilly was well-known to traders' horse-drawn vans and, funnily enough, the horses were almost as knowing as the drivers! They always stopped at the appropriate houses without being reined in and some begged unshamedly at those homes where the housewives had given them crusts of bread! They knew when they had reached the end of their rounds, too, because they turned back without being told to and set off home at a smart pace.

We never saw motor vehicles in the early 1920s, apart from the new 'shaker' hard-tyred buses which began running along Wolseley Road. Swilly was then on the edge of the town with lush countryside to the north and the east. Rural Weston Mill, just further along, as you approached St Budeaux, had its unspoilt beauty while, further out still, Woodland and Budshead Woods were a magnet for energetic youngsters.

In one way and another, then, Swilly was a very popular area in which to live. Many of the tenancies were taken by Navy men, technicians or craftsmen in the Dockyard, tradesmen and policemen. The man who lived next door to us was a signals technician warrant officer in the Navy; he was the first chap around our way to own a radio set, then regarded as a great marvel. He built it himself, juggling around with various coils, circuits and aerials.

Leisure pursuits were no problem at all. With such large areas of open space we were outdoors a good deal of our time, never at a loss to know what to do. I have the feeling that today's young people don't experience anything like the true freedom and enjoyment that my generation did, even though we were supposed to be 'deprived' by current standards. Continual games of cricket and football were then the order of the day, even if it did result in the grass eventually vanishing.

Marbles was another favourite, but not just *any* marbles! We were true connoisseurs in those days. One type of marbles, made of baked clay covered with enamel, was despised by most people since they were too easily broken and too light, anyway, for the many manoeuvres which the game demanded. Most of us preferred 'stonies', a marble made from real, natural stone, attractively marked and solid. Or there were 'aggies', natural marble or limestone, and 'glassies', which included a beautiful swirl of coloured glass in the centre. A Devonport shop, Wood and Tozer's, carried drawerfuls of marbles and a visit to that emporium was an exciting experience.

Many boys were adept at making themselves a trolley, which became their inseparable companion. This called for a visit to the local Co-op to buy a stout wooden box for a couple of pennies, preferably a soap box. Then followed calls on relatives, or a visit to the tip at Camel's Head, to search for discarded pram wheels and axles. The construction of a trolley required only nails, a hammer and a willing assistant and the result, after a couple of days hard work, would be a serviceable vehicle, guaranteed to stand up to all manner of wear and tear.

Girls and boys had their own games groups and seldom joined up, would you believe! The former used skipping ropes and various bits and pieces with which to play 'shop'. Another favourite game was ship tops. In this, the whip was a short stick with about two feet of Co-op white parcel string, which was mighty tough. The boys favoured flyers, which had smaller and lighter tops and flew long distances – still spinning – when whipped. Many boys had huge iron hoops, often up to five feet in diameter, propelled by a stick.

I don't think people today realize how 'countrified' Swilly was seventy years ago. When we moved in a Corporation house there in 1920 Wolseley Road had only just been built; before that it was a pleasant country lane bordered by large trees and open fields, and running from Oak Villa, at Camel's Head – which then had its own police station, by the way. You could even travel into the centre of Plymouth by sea, as well as train or tram! Camel's Head was then fully tidal and, provided you knew the tide times, you were safe enough in a small boat, even if it did take a long time. But not everyone was in such a hurry in those days!

Those who preferred to stay on dry land used the GWR railcar at St Budeaux or Keyham, while the LSWR called at Weston Mill and Camel's Head halts. The trams each had their own conductors; some of the really funny ones were a little like today's TV compères without being so slick. They got to know their regular passengers and used to ask them such questions as, 'How's your leg today?' or 'Has your husband found work yet?' It built up a tremendous rapport between them and us, so much so that we called them by their first names. A lot of backchat went on between them and the female passengers who often would dissolve into giggles. Many of the elderly folk looked forward to all this fun and carry-on because an outing by tram became almost a social occasion. It's not like that any more, is it?

Fields each end of Brunel's bridge at Camel's Head (looking south). But urban sprawl can be seen in the top right-hand corner.
▼

'Open day' on H.M.S. *Mount Edgecumbe* in the early 1900s. This training ship was moored on the Tamar from 1877 to 1920; homeless and destitute boys were taught sea-craft aboard it. It was a well-known local sight.

One of the railcars that both the G.W.R. and the L.S.W.R. ran around the suburbs of Plymouth and into the centre.

Of course, trips into town were rather special occasions. We didn't have to go unless we wanted to shop at the really large departmental stores, like Spooner's, Yeo's and, for those who could afford it, Popham's. We had a number of small shops within a short walking distance away, including post offices, chemists, bakers, off-licences, fishmongers, greengrocers, ironmongers and several sweet shops. When you see what little in this line is left now you'll see how well off we felt.

In those days, all the children in Swilly looked forward to colourful annual events, invariably concluded by a large free tea. The Royal Naval Barracks held sports every summer, and we lads scrounged around the Navy men trying to get a free ticket. These were blue and pink and one of the colours entitled you to a free tea – and what a treat that was! We were served by naval ratings who stuffed us full of delicious food and the usual arrangement was that if you couldn't eat any more, then you took it home.

— DEVONPORT: —
guns and butter

The oblong shape of the old Devonport has been changed dramatically over the last forty-five years, and so has its character. The heart of the town was removed when the Dockyard expanded westwards and, by erecting a boundary wall down Chapel Street, effectively cut the north off from the south. Devonport's jugular veins of Fore, Catherine, Tavistock, Cumberland and St Aubyn Streets were cut out while the west side of James Street, and the north side of Duke Street, were removed and replaced by a block wall which links up with Chapel Street.

Plymouth planners began changing the face of Devonport long before the German bombers pounded it into rubble fifty years ago. Demolition became the order of the day after the land at Mutton Cove and Richmond Walk had been bought; the residents were moved out and their cottages cleared away. Shops in Prospect Row, Cornwall Street and Cannon Street were demolished, and replaced by flats. After the town had been battered by the bombs the planners got to work again, deciding to sweep away what was left of many old and familiar streets. Just four shops were allowed at the end of George Street as a bizarre token to the several hundred which had gone.

A present-day view of the area from Devonport monument gives little aesthetic pleasure unless you look upwards and outwards towards the freedom and the freshness of Mount Edgecumbe.

Ron Smith, born and bred in Devonport, has spent many hours listening to elderly people who grew up in the town in the early years of the century. Much of the stockpile of information he gleaned came from his grandfather, Mr John Bromley, who was born in Richmond Walk in 1879 and died nearly thirty years ago. His family had settled in generations before that, however, the first recorded death being at Ravelin Cottage, near St Aubyn Street, in 1846.

In these reminiscences he recalls a Devonport that often was very noisy, with crowded streets teeming with children at play. The steel rims of cartwheels trundled over the granite cobbles mixing with the sound of horses' hoofs. Close to the Dockyard wall was the constant noise of ships being built: the racket of the rivet guns, the din of steel clanking on steel, ships bells and sirens sounding across the Hamoaze. They were sights and sounds which he took for granted from an early age.

On Sundays, six churches would ring out their bells, accompanied by the chimes of the market clock. Four-horse work teams pulled coal and timber from the quays at Mutton Cove. The brewery drays, brasses shining, made deliveries to the seventeen beer retailers in the street, where the rattle of bottles and the thump of beer barrels rolling along the pavements was a familiar sound. The sawdust seller brought sacks of dust from the timber mills for inn floors; salt sellers, too, were a popular sight, not only for the shopkeepers but also for people to rub into meat, bacon and fish in an attempt to preserve it longer. Added to this was the 'block ice' cart, the coalman and the chopped wood merchant mingling with the ponies and traps constantly moving about the area.

Ron Smith recalls that with so many horses, the roads had to receive regular sweeping and many men were employed for this purpose.

These sweepings from Devonport streets were loaded into barges at Mutton Cove and North Corner. From there it was taken up the Tamar where the contents were unloaded by farmers to spread over the many fruit fields.

The crowded Hamoaze from Devonport Column. This congested town area, devastated in the blitz, and followed up by the massive post-war dock extensions, is now quite unrecognizable.

▲
Excavations for the new Keyham Dock extension, which was opened in 1907. The Dockyard employed 20000 men at its height and, during the inter-war years, accounted for a quarter of Plymouth's workforce.

He also recalls a time when life for most people in Devonport was hard, when poverty was commonplace.

Devonport's living conditions could be appalling. Even by the end of the First World War the older properties often were in a very bad state of repair. Many old houses had limestone paving right through the ground-floor passages; even the odd kitchen – always referred to as the parlour – did, and it made them very cold in winter. Gas mantles in the main rooms were the only form of lighting until the 1920s apart from candles or smoky oil lamps. Old black-cast iron gas stoves, or coal burning ranges, formed the means of cooking and I remember that it was one of the children's tasks to clean them with stove blacking – a very messy job.

Few homes had an internal water supply, most of them drawing water from a lone tap situated in the courtyards, which were usually of limestone flags. At the end of the courtyard would be a single toilet, and it was not unusual for eight families to share it. Most had a fixed wooden plank seat and doors with gaps at both tops and bottoms. On dark winter evenings it was often the duty of a brother to escort his sister to such a toilet. For most families in Devonport, though, night-time functions were carried out in a slop bucket in the children's bedroom. Brothers and sisters, regardless of age, shared not only the same room but also the same bed.

The launch of H.M.S. *Weston super Mare* from the Dockyard on 23 July 1932. Launches of naval boats have been a familiar sight in Devonport for nearly 300 years.

'Turning out time' from Devonport Dockyard in a late afternoon in 1910. Sam Tremain's carriages were always waiting. The cashiers' office was just inside the Dockyard gate. The town was set alight when thousands of men poured out of the Yard, on their way home.

▲

North Corner. The first houses on what was to become Plymouth Dock were built here in the 1690s. The lower half of Cornwall Street, which ran down at right angles to the river front, housed mainly boating families who had lived there for generations.

Many people still sigh for what they have convinced themselves were the 'good old days', but my family remembers that vermin was common in most houses, much to the satisfaction of the huge cat population. In fact, if you lived next door to a bakery you could expect your ground-floor room to be walking with cockroaches at night.

Families were large, with sixteen children not unknown; two of my aunts each had ten. Clothes were handed down the line or passed on from friend to friend. Jumpers, dresses and smocks often were made by a grandmother and many old photographs tend to reflect the difficulties parents faced over clothing their children. In general, it was drab, tending to be grey or brown with only the white blouse or aprons giving any freshness.

Boys wore fairly heavy boots, never shoes. These were studded on their bottoms with the heels plated to give maximum wear. Long trousers were 'out' until you were about thirteen and long home-knitted woollen socks were the order of the day. I wonder how many young mothers today could sit down with three steel needles and knit a pair of stockings? Girls wore long dresses of heavy warm material covered by a long smock or apron. For very young girls it was often a case of bare feet and no underwear, summer or winter. One way and another it is hardly surprising that a welcome roundsman to families in this 'poverty trap' was the familiar rag-and-bone man, travelling around with a pony and cart. He offered cheap bargains or exchanged clothing. Small families and shopkeepers managed much better and their off-spring were better dressed.

For all that, there was pride among poor families. Something special was kept for Sunday School or an important occasion, and a beautiful piece of new ribbon often was a young girl's pride and joy.

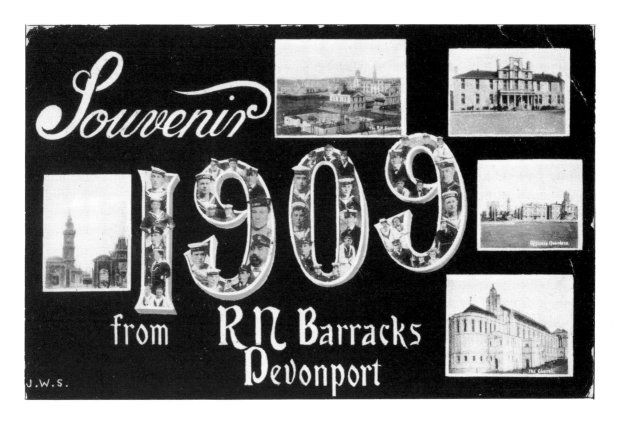

STREETS AND MARKETS

Mrs Marjorie Laxton, whose maiden name was Toms, was born in Duke Street, Devonport, and later the family moved to George Street, remaining there for twenty-eight years. She grew up in a lively, closely-knit Devonport where it seemed that every child went off to the market for a dollop of cream.

It was a joy. The fruit and flower, poultry and vegetable stalls, were always full. My mother took me there every Saturday morning to see a Mrs Shore, who came over from Butspill Farm, Bere Alston. This lady, with her black dress and large white apron, supplied us with butter, cream and eggs; she sold apples by the hundred. The butter market was upstairs, where the pats were all laid out in a line for neat display. Each carried a picture – some a sheaf of corn or a cow, say. Just inside the Cumberland Street entrance to the market was the toffee stall. This was a great attraction, with huge slabs of toffee arranged in rows, some creamy and others with fruit and nut.

A lady used to break the slabs with a little toffee hammer, and it tasted delicious. Traders took a great pride in their goods. I used to love going into the grocery stores, such as William Haddy's, Alford's or Miles'. I remember the stationers Horns and Miller in Fore Street, near a sixpenny bazaar where glass and china, basins and rows of yellow mixing bowls were arranged around the floor. Further along was a music shop called Morris's. During the first Devonport carnival people were asked to guess the number of needles in their window, the prize being a bedroom suite.

▲
With tens of thousands of sailors based in Devonport, or 'Guzz', souvenir cards were a basic necessity of life. Sent to a Miss Gifford of Newton Abbot, this one was written by 'E.E.' and states: 'I passed my swimming test and was vaccinated on Monday, so my leave will be stopped until better. Remember me to Ethel.'

Fore Street in the 1920s. At this time the street was graced by many of the larger 'chains', three cinemas and a host of pubs. ▶

Pembroke Street was a very busy thoroughfare, with almost one out of four businesses a public house. I remember that when the naval men came ashore, either at Mount Wise or Mutton Cove, their first visit would be to the little post office leading into James Street where they would buy postcards for their folks to say when they could be expected to arrive at home. Then, many of them spent their time, and a good deal of their money, in the pubs, after which they would make their way to 'Aggie' Weston's in Fore Street, where they could sober up. Right opposite that large brick building, the Dockyard entrance, was an oilskin shop, where sou'-westers and sea boots were hung out.

In the corner of St Stephen's Lane was a lovely dairy run by Viggers; I used to get a large white jug of milk for a penny there.

Mrs Laxton also recalled the larger stores such as Boolds which stretched from Devonport Market up towards York Street. Tozer's was another large drapery store fronting Malborough Street into Granby Street. Sir Clifford Tozer, owner of the store, later became leader of the local Conservative Party on the City Council, an alderman and the Lord Mayor.

Boolds had a Michelin Tyre figure in their window which was inflated and moved up and down. Its name was Billy-by-Bendum and he was quite an attraction. Tozer's built its reputation on the letters SPQR, which stood for 'small profits for quick returns'.

For the young May Cole, born in Devonport in the early years of the century, excursions to Plymouth were rare, perhaps three a year, one of them to see the pantomime at the Palace Theatre, and another to take an annual saunter on the Hoe.

There was no real point in going to Plymouth when we had everything we needed in Devonport, including theatres, cinemas, lovely shops and that wonderful market. Most of its produce, such as eggs and butter, came up from Cornwall the same day it was sold, including fresh chickens, which we took home and plucked, usually late on Saturday night. The market stayed open until nine o'clock, anyway, and so did many of the shops. Fore Street was the main mecca, with its two sides of smart shops which were as good as anything in Plymouth.

Marlborough Street is still in existence. Once it ranked second only in importance to Fore Street.
◀

Tavistock Street, shortly before the First World War, showing Boold's, a large drapery store, and, further up on the right, The Alhambra Theatre.
▼

Tavistock Street, Devonport.

E 31871

Completely different in outlook and feel from the tightly packed dockyard town was Plymouth, in those days a separate borough. Mrs Laxton remembers travelling there by tram. The Devonport tram took people from the Fore Street terminus through Chapel Street, stopping at Cumberland Gardens, and then past Raglan Barracks.

It stopped in Edgecumbe Street, Stonehouse, to pick up passengers, eventually ending its run at Derry's clock, this being the Plymouth terminus.

I remember the fascination of watching the conductor changing the trolley arm over to the other overhead wire for the return journey. If he happened to be short it could be tricky; the arm, being heavy, could swing and spark until eventually it clicked onto the wire. My bedtime was at 5.45 and, as evening drew on, the trams rattled down over the hill toward the Ha'penny Gate on Stonehouse Bridge. I used to lie in bed watching the coloured sparks which seemed to sprout from the tops of the trees: red, green and blue and all caused by the trolley arm passing points on the overhead wire.

A tram crossing Stonehouse Bridge and Ha'penny Gate on its way into Plymouth. The first electric trams ran in 1899 from the centre of Plymouth to Prince Rock and, later, Compton. Devonport followed two years later, extending to the growing areas of Millbridge, Stoke, Keyham and Camel's Head. Over 100 trams were in service at any one time during the peak years of the early 1900s. ▶

HALFPENNY GATE, STONEHOUSE

AN ANATOMY OF DEVONPORT

The face of Devonport has been changed greatly over the past fifty years and there are many who would say that there has been no improvement. Ron Smith has done some exhaustive research on the appearance of some of the town's major areas as they used to be.

Ker Street: a street of elegance

This was the street of the hansom cab and of smartly-dressed people. Conversely, it was also the street through which wicker caskets on pram wheels, containing a corpse, were solemnly pushed to the nearest cemetery.

Ker Street was the last major area to be developed in Devonport; it was built on the brow of a hill that sloped southwards to limestone cliffs facing the Tamar.

An old windmill stood on the brow and the hill itself was quarried out between Ker Street and Richmond Walk, providing limestone and dunrock.

Ker Street was developed in the 1820s when the road was laid with Cornish granite cobbles; large and elegant houses lined the street, many with ornate iron rails in front of them. In some, limestone steps led down to a basement door. Solid, wooden and panelled front doors opened inwards to reveal coloured and picture-tiled hallways and inner doors, many of which supported beautiful coloured glass; there were walled gardens at the rear of each building. Pride of place in Ker Street was taken by the Guildhall with a fire station on its south side and a police station at the rear. At the east base of the commemorative Column, erected in 1824, was the British School for Girls, later to become the Ker Street Infants School. The Zion Hall headquarters of the Salvation Army was adjacent to the Oddfellows' Hall, which included a library and reading rooms.

Ker Street, with the Guildhall at the end, the Odd Fellows' Hall on the right and, behind that, Devonport Column.
◀

Cumberland Street

Here was a street which covered most household needs. I used to run errands for my grandparents into most of the shops and it has left me with lasting memories of the kind people who served from behind the counters. There was a small park in Cumberland Gardens, with Martin's, the bakers, on the south side. The smell was of bread and cakes in the early mornings, and the baking of apple squares, topped with a sprinkling of sugar. It was a real childhood delight I have never forgotten. By mid-morning the smell of pasties being cooked drifted downwards; next to that particular shop was Roberts the newsagent, always popular with us boys because of its Beano and Dandy comics. A hairdressers', Dr McCombe's surgery and the Lord Beresford Inn were next in line.

Prouts' the chemists was on the corner. It had a smell all of its own and its windows displayed large glass containers of coloured water. On the next corner was Dolton and Aunger, the dairy, with large blocks of butter and white lard, and sometimes a whole cheese, on the marble counters. When cut, the butter would be rolled between two ribbed pats into the shape of a log and finally embossed with a cow before it was wrapped. Milk would be ladled from large urns into a wide-neck bottle which would then be sealed with a cardboard top. At No.21

Cumberland Street after the War. Although it is run-down here the architecture reveals the former prosperity of the street. ▶

Cumberland Street, was Kelly's fruit shop from where families collected their weekly orders. Sometimes Mr Kelly would sell blackberries – you could pick anything up to 21lb at Maker Heights. My grandfather used to row us from Mutton Cove to Cremyll and then we'd walk it. I used the money for the 'flicks' and grandad used to buy some twist or pigtail tobacco.

A little further down the hill, and a favourite shop of mine, was Humphrey's which sold fish and chips. Nearby was a fruit shop, Lamerton's, where you could often get six spotty apples for a penny. Large, heavy delivery push-bikes stood outside most shops, with prominent baskets positioned over the front wheels and a metal nameplate under the crossbar. Errand boys used to deliver goods to customers free of charge.

St Aubyn Street: the professional street

Most people had to use this street at sometime or other because it contained the registrars' offices for births, marriages and deaths; many others journeyed through it by tram to Fore Street. The houses were large and varied in style, and mainly occupied by professional people. There were, for instance, ten solicitors' offices, four dental surgeries and four doctors' consulting rooms.

Fine early Victorian buildings along St Aubyn Street in this post-war photograph. Once the street housed Devonport's professional classes.
◀

79

The Devonport Blind Institution also was in St Aubyn Street, producing many types of baskets for sale. There was also an undertakers, a bookmakers, a Co-op shop, a chemist and two wine merchants. Several of the large houses were used as better-class rented apartments.

Richmond Walk

The changes along the stretch of the Tamar between Mutton Cove and Stonehouse Creek have been dramatic in the last sixty years. For instance a collection of cottages and small quays, with slips of granite emerging from the sea, stood where the new marina now is. These were demolished and a large new railway quay took their place. Coal wharves and a large fertiliser plant came into being and cargo boats become regular callers. Another small community of dwellings, known as Victoria Cottages, stood on the site of the car-park; at one time, these adjoined the Royal Clarence Baths.

Below Blagdon's boatyard was the town swimming bath, and a nearby open pebble beach provided a sunny spot for local people – it was common for children to swim in the nude there, and no one minded a bit.

The little stone cottage built there is part of the Blagdon family home. It was erected in the 1840s and its correct name is Rose Cottage. A small limestone quay stood in front of the cottage at one time – it is now under Mr Blagdon's workshop and can still be seen from the beach. Two other cottages, known as Bromleys, were adjacent until the mid 1950s. One was put up in the 1840s but the larger was built in 1861 by my great-great grandfather, Mr Benjamin Bromley.

He bought the smaller property from the lord of the manor and from these three dwellings a boat hire business was operated. When he died in 1900 the business passed to his younger daughter, Clara, and it was there, in 1879, that my grandfather, John Bromley, was born. In the early 1920s a small hut was built at the back of the main cottage and this was used as a sweet shop. The boundary wall separating these properties from Richmond Walk is government property. The opening in the wall to allow access down the steps to all three cottages meant the owners had to pay an annual token fee to the Admiralty; in fact, Mr Blagdon pays an annual fee to this day.

The Admiral's Pier stands on the original landing slabs laid down in 1820 to give access for high ranking officers to Government House, and a serviceman was on duty there until the 1950s. When you step out of the guard house and cross the walk you are confronted by a limestone archway and two flights of granite steps which lead up to Mount Wise. A coal merchant used to do business on the waterfront, stocks being brought by sea from London and South Wales; today the men's changing rooms stand on this spot.

Mutton Cove

When the Dockyard finally had expanded southwards by 1780 its boundary wall left a little inlet which allowed southern access into the old town of Dock. Local limestone was quarried and, with Cornish granite, a small harbour was formed. On the south-west corner two landing stages of steps were constructed, one on the outside quay and the other just inside the harbour entrance. A public landing slip was built at the centre and north side of the harbour, and the original steps are in good condition today, if a little worn. The outer quay's long arm was known as Benevolent Quay and there was no pier until the 1900s. Several little houses were constructed behind the harbour, and a granite cobble road was

An early shot of Mutton Cove harbour, with the old houses of the 'Cove people' behind.

Part of the Devonport waterfront, Mutton Cove landing stage was one of the earliest bases for steam excursions, much in favour by generations of local people. It was also in demand by yacht and boat owners, and still is a favourite gathering spot on warm weekends.

built running towards the south-west corner of the quay; it was the only landing space along the waterfront.

About twenty properties had formed a little village snuggling under the Dockyard wall. The first public-house built near the centre of the village was the Mount Edgecumbe Inn; this was followed by the Mutton Cove Hotel and the Waterman's Arms.

The majority of the people crowding into these densely-packed houses were watermen and their families. Many were illiterate but they were certainly professional when it came to handling their sturdy boats, and their profound knowledge of the river currents would not be found in any book. They were a waterside people and they touted for their trade – there was real pride in being one of 'The Cove people'. And the women in the family could pull an oar as well as any man.

Throughout the summer the quay walls from King Billy's statue to the end of the children's boating pool were often lined with people standing shoulder to shoulder, and all holding a fishing pole. A shout would go up of 'Mackerel up the wall', and poles would jerk upwards, snatching gleaming silver mackerel out of the sea up on to the quay. In those days the swimming pools were nearly always open and youngsters would chase the shoals right to the end of the baths. Reels were not the order of the day – just a piece of wood tied near the end of the cane to hold a length of cord would do. That was the Cove people all over – not the world's most sophisticated, but always ready to improvise, and enjoying the work as much as the leisure.

CHILDHOOD IN DEVONPORT

For May Cole, the most vivid memories of her childhood in Devonport were of the outdoor life and the marvellous opportunities for swimming. The Mount Wise pools were particularly popular.

Nearly everyone used the pools. We didn't need to go over to the Hoe when we had our own, right at hand. My brother, who was a sailor, became one of the finest swimmers in Devon and he started off at Mount Wise.

Mutton Cove, almost adjacent, was another favourite haunt – particularly for May, since her uncle ran boats from there to Cremyll.

We used to go right up the river with him to places like Calstock. Sometimes we swam part of the distance behind the boat. It was nothing to me because, by seven, I was a proficient swimmer.

Her parents, Mr and Mrs Westlake, lived in St James Street, and that's where she grew up. Father was in the Navy and so was away from home for long periods but life was always full for young May.

The only part I didn't enjoy was school. Many of my contemporaries insist that they did, but I honestly wonder how much of this is make-believe. Certainly the discipline was strict. You had to be punctual and dress well. My uniform, if you can call it that, consisted of high brown boots, a navy pleated skirt and blouse.

What else did the children who teemed in the streets of Devonport do with their time, once they were out of school? Ron Smith gives some clues, both from his own childhood, and from the younger days of the generation before him.

▲

Mount Wise has been, and
still is, a great favourite for
recreation. There is a fine
view to the King William
Victualling Yard across the
river.

In those days, not only was there no television or radio, but 'talking films' were a
fantasy of the future. There wasn't the money for long trips anywhere much, yet
the word boredom wasn't in common use. Certainly, children did not go around
daubing graffiti on lavatory walls or 'mugging' old ladies of their savings.
Pleasures were simple and, in their own way, creative. The size of the limestone
paving slabs made them ideal for games of 'hop and step'. Numerals were first
chalked on the slabs and, by pitching a stone into the selected square, a child
would advance until all the numbers had been covered. If the stone landed in the
wrong square, or on a dividing line, they had to wait for another turn. Another
favourite with all children was swings, with a rope thrown over the arms of the
lamp-posts, though everyone ran for it if a policeman hove into sight.

A popular summer's game was 'Cherry Pips', fruit being abundant, and cheap
from the Tamar Valley. Squares were cut out of a piece of cardboard and each
window was given a number. The board was placed against a building wall and
each contestant retreated to the kerb. Then the skill of flicking a cherry stone
through a window would be tested with a score being given after perhaps a
dozen stones had been used. In the summer there was free swimming at
Richmond Walk, both from the beach and the pool now covered by Blagdon's
boatyard or, for some, from the landing slip in Mutton Cove Harbour. Groups of
children with a few jam sandwiches and coffee, bottles of water or cold tea, went
to the grass slopes of Mount Wise or the Brickfields for a picnic.

▲
Devonport Park was laid out in 1858. Its thirty-seven acres included two band-stands at one time, where military bands from the local garrisons played to appreciative audiences.

An early photograph of the Royal Naval Barracks. Barrack blocks were first built here in 1889, providing quarters for men who had previously been based in old ship hulks moored in the Hamoaze. Previously known as H.M.S. *Vivid*, the name was changed to H.M.S. *Drake* in 1934. ▶

I'm told that in the early years of this century some of the more venturesome children would make for the Richmond Walk limestone quarries, then no longer in use and known to all as 'The Rockies'. At the bottom of the 'cut' from Devonport Hill was a very large flat-faced rock tilted at an angle of forty-five degrees and worn smooth with time. If you climbed around the rails to the actual rock it made an ideal slide. From this north-east end of the quarry it was possible to walk up the old thirty-foot defence trench – abandoned in 1860 – under Devonport Hill Road, and on through the trench into the Brickfields. Many trenches were dug there during the First World War and groups of children used to love to sneak past the soldiers on duty and scramble into them. They were nearly always caught because of the noise they made shouting to each other.

All in all, children certainly were not bored for want of something to do. Families in general were pretty poor throughout Devonport and life was hard for the children, with none of the modern comforts, not to say expensive amusements which are taken granted today. But it was a time of adventure and imagination and children were allowed to be children.

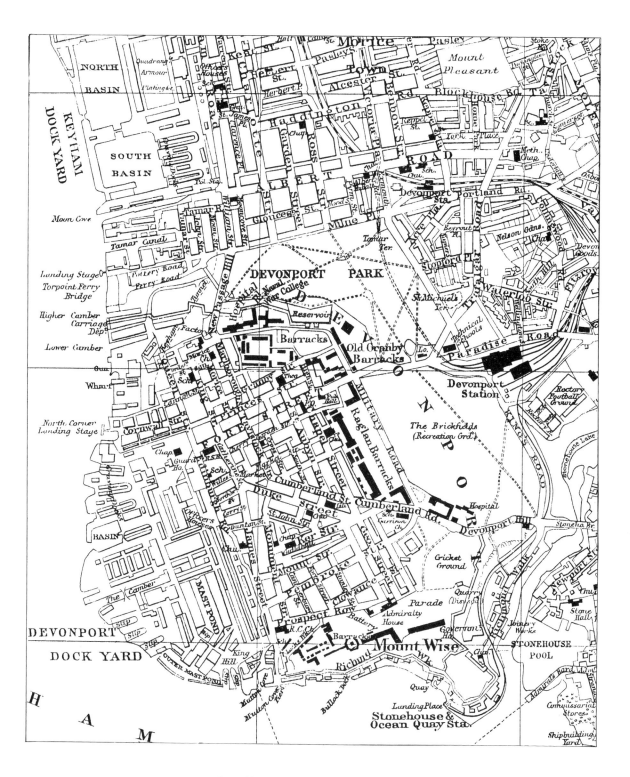

Central Devonport from a pre-war street map.

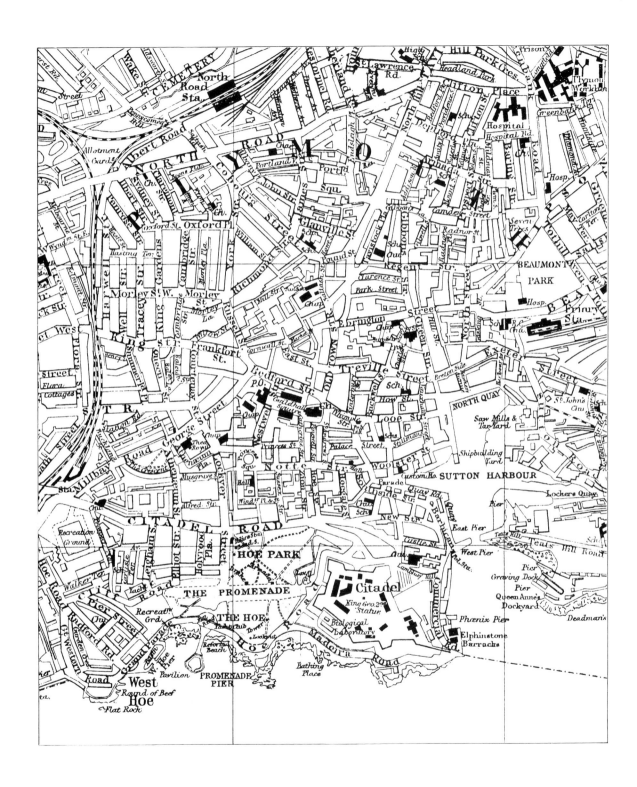

Central Plymouth from a pre-war street map.

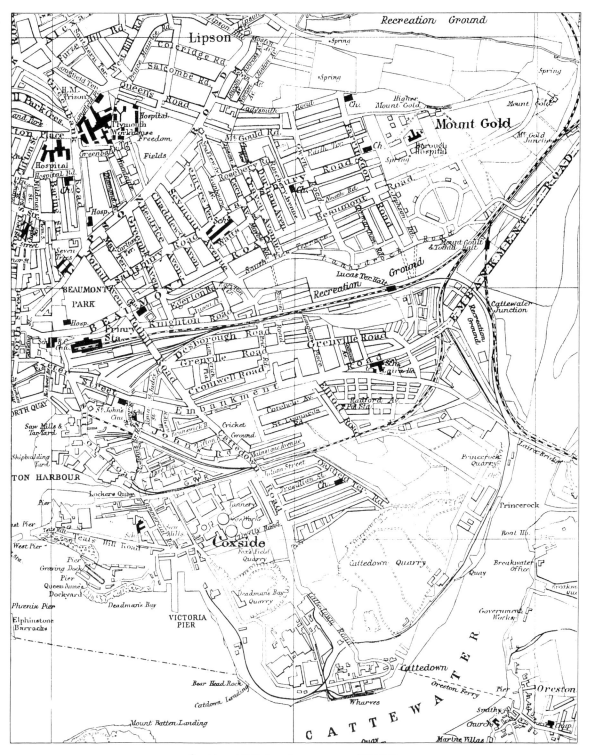

Coxside and Cattedown from a pre-war street map.

PLYMOUTH, STONEHOUSE, AND DEVONPORT.

The three towns in the second half of the nineteenth century.